THE ITALIAN TRAVELMATE

compiled by
LEXUS
with
Annelisa Franchini

RICHARD DREW PUBLISHING
Glasgow

RICHARD DREW PUBLISHING LTD.
6 CLAIRMONT GARDENS
GLASGOW G3 7LW
SCOTLAND

First Published 1982
First Reprint April 1982
Second Reprint May 1984
New Edition 1986

ISBN 0 904002 77 2

Printed and bound in Great Britain by
Cox & Wyman Ltd.

YOUR TRAVELMATE
gives you one single easy-to-use list of words and phrases to help you communicate in Italian.

Built into this list are:
– Travel Tips with facts and figures which provide valuable information
– Italian words you'll see on signs and notices
– typical replies to some of the things you might want to say.

There is a menu reader on pages 70–71, the Italian alphabet is given on page 127 and numbers on page 128.

Your TRAVELMATE also tells you how to pronounce Italian. Just read the pronunciations as though they were English and you will communicate – although you might not sound like a native speaker.

If no pronunciation is given then the word itself can be pronounced as though it were English. And sometimes only part of a word or phrase needs a pronunciation guide. Vowels given in italics show which part of a word to stress.

ITALIA
GERMANIA
AUSTRIA
SVIZZERA
TICINO
JUGOSLAVIA
Stresa
Piemonte
Torino
Milano
Lombardia
Veneto
Venezia
Trieste
Genova
Bologna
Romagna
Rimini
San Marino
Ancona
Marche
Pisa
Firenze (Florence)
Toscana
MONACO
Mar Ligure
Elba
Corsica
Ajaccio
Lazio
Roma
Abruzzo
MARE ADRIATICO
Bari
Puglia
Campania
Napoli
VESUVIO
Taranto
Capri
Lucania
Sardegna
MARE TIRRENO
Cagliari
Calabria
Mar Ionio
Palermo
Messina
ETNA
Catania
Sicilia
MARE MEDITERRANEO
Tunis
TUNISIA
MALTA

a, an un, una [oon, *oo*-nah]
800 lire a litre ottocento lire al litro [ot-toh-*chen*-toh *lee*-ray . . .]
abdomen l'addome [ad-*doh*-may]
aboard a bordo
about: is the manager about? c'è il direttore? [cheh eel dee-rayt-*toh*-ray]
about 15 circa quindici [*cheer*-kah *kween*-dee-chee]
about 2 o'clock verso le due [. . . *doo*-ay]
above sopra
abroad all'estero [al-*les*-tay-roh]
absolutely! certo! [*chayr*-toh]
accelerator l'acceleratore [la-chay-lay-ra-*toh*-ray]
accendere i fari *switch on headlights*
accept accettare [a-chet-*tah*-ray]
accident un incidente [een-chee-*den*-tay]
there's been an accident è successo un incidente [eh soo-*ches*-soh . . .]
accommodation un posto da dormire [. . . dor-*mee*-ray]
we need accommodation for three c'è [cheh] posto da dormire per tre?
» *TRAVEL TIP: information can be obtained from the local tourist office, called 'Pro Loco'*
accountant un ragioniere [ra-jon-*yeh*-ray]
accurate accur*a*to
ache un dolore [doh-*loh*-ray]
my back aches mi fa mal la schiena [mee fah mal lah skee-*ay*-nah]
ACI = *Automobil Club d'Italia: like our AA or RAC*
acqua potabile *drinking water*

across attraverso
how do we get across? come attraversiamo? [k*oh*-may . . .]
adaptor una spina intermedia [sp*ee*-nah een-ter-m*ay*-dee-ah]
adjust aggiustare [ah-joos-t*ah*-ray]
address l'indirizzo [een-dee-r*ee*t-tzoh]
will you give me your address? mi dai il tuo indirizzo? [mee d*ah*-ee . . .]
admission l'entrata
advance: can we book in advance? possiamo prenotare? [. . .–tah-ray]
advert un annuncio [an-n*oo*n-choh]
afraid: I'm afraid I don't know purtroppo non so
I'm afraid so purtroppo sì [. . . see]
I'm afraid not no, mi spiace [no mee spee-*ah*-chay]
after: after you dopo di lei [. . . dee lay]
after 3 o'clock dopo le tre [. . . lay tray]
afternoon il pomeriggio [po-may-r*ee*-joh]
this afternoon questo pomeriggio
in the afternoon nel pomeriggio
good afternoon *(from morning till mid-afternoon)* buon giorno [bwon j*o*r-noh]
(after that) buona sera [bw*o*-nah s*ay*-rah]
aftershave il dopobarba
again anc*o*ra
against contro
age l'età [ay-t*ah*]
under age minorenne [mee-no-r*e*n-nay]
it takes ages ci vogliono anni [chee vol-yoh-noh *a*n-nee]
ago: a week ago una settimana fa
it wasn't long ago non tanto tempo fa
how long ago was that? quanto tempo fa?
agree: I agree sono d'accordo
it doesn't agree with me non mi fa bene [non mee fah b*ay*-nay]

air l'aria [*ah*-ree-ah]
by air in aereo [een ah-*eh*-ray-oh]
by airmail per posta aerea [. . . ah-*eh*-ray-ah]
with air-conditioning con l'aria condizionata [. . . kon-dee-tzee-o-*nah*-tah]
airport l'aeroporto [ah-ay-ro-*por*-toh]
alarm l'allarme [–may]
alarm clock le sveglia [*svay*l-yah]
alcohol l'alcol [*a*l-kol]
is it alcoholic? è alcolico? [eh al-*ko*-lee-koh]
alive vivo [*vee*-voh]
is he still alive? è ancora vivo? [eh . . .]
all tutto [*too*t-toh]
all night tutta la notte [–tay]
that's all wrong è tutto sbagliato [eh . . . sbal-*yah*-toh]
all right va bene [. . . *bay*-nay]
I'm all right sto bene
that's all è tutto
thank you – not at all grazie – prego [*grah*-tzee ay *pray*-goh]
allergic allergico [al-*ler*-jee-koh]
I'm allergic to sono allergico a
allowed permesso
is it allowed? è permesso?
it's not allowed è vietato [eh vee-ay-*tah*-toh]
allow me mi permetta [mee . . .]
almost quasi [*kwah*-see]
alone solo
did you come here alone? è venuto solo? [eh . . .]
leave me alone mi lasci stare [mee *lah*-shee *stah*-ray]
Alps: the Alps le Alpi [lay-*a*l-pee]
already già [djah]
also anche [*a*n-kay]
alt *halt*
alternator l'alternatore [–*toh*-ray]
although sebbene [seb-*beh*-nay]

altogether in tutto [een *too*t-toh]
what does that make altogether? quant'è in tutto? [kwan-*teh* . . .]
always sempre [*se*m-pray]
a.m. di mattina [dee mat-*tee*-nah]
ambassador l'ambasciatore [am-ba-sha-*toh*-ray]
ambulance un'ambulanza [am-boo-*la*n-tzah]
get an ambulance! chiamate un'ambulanza! [kee-a-*mah*-tay . . .]
» TRAVEL TIP: *Phone 113 anywhere in Italy*
America l'America [a-*may*-ree-kah]
American americano
among fra
anchor l'ancora [*a*n-ko-rah]
ancient Rome Roma Antica [. . . an-*tee*-kah]
and e [ay]
angry sec*ca*to
I'm very angry about it sono molto seccato al riguardo [. . . ree-gw*a*r-doh]
please don't get angry non si arrabbi [non see ar-*ra*b-bee]
animal un animale [a-nee-*mah*-lay]
ankle la caviglia [ka-*vee*l-yah]
anniversary: it's our anniversary è il nostro annivers*a*rio [eh . . .]
annoy: he's annoying me mi sta seccando [mee . . .]
it's very annoying è molto seccante [eh m*o*l-toh sayk-*ka*n-tay]
anorak la giacca a vento [*ja*k-kah . . .]
another: can we have another room? potremmo avere un'altra camera? [. . . a-*vay*-ray . . .]
another beer, please un'altra birra, per favore [. . . fa-*voh*-ray]
answer *(noun)* una risposta
what was his answer? qual'è stata la sua risposta?

there was no answer nessuno ha risposto [. . . ah . . .]
antifreeze l'antigelo [an-tee-*jay*-loh]
any: have you any bananas/butter? avete delle banane/del burro? [a-*vay*-tay *day*l-lay ba-*nah*-nay . . .]
I haven't got any non ne ho [non nay o]
anybody qualcuno [kwal-*koo*-noh]
I can't see anybody non vedo nessuno [. . . *vay*-doh . . .]
anything qualcosa
anything will do va bene tutto [vah *bay*-nay *toot*-toh]
I don't want anything non voglio niente [non *vol*-yoh nee-*en*-tay]
aperitif un aperitivo [–*tee*-voh]
aperto *open*
apology una scusa [*skoo*-sah]
please accept my apologies mi scusi [mee . . .]
I want an apology desidero le sue scuse [day-*see*-day-roh lay *soo*-ay . . .]
appendicitis l'appendicite [ap-pen-dee-*chee*-tay]
appetite l'appetito [ap-pay-*tee*-toh]
I've lost my appetite non ho più appetito [. . . o pew . . .]
apple una mela
application form il modulo [*mo*-doo-loh]
appointment: can I make an appointment? posso avere un appuntamento? [. . . a-*vay*-ray . . .]
apricot un'albicocca
April aprile [a-*pree*-lay]
aqualung l'autorespiratore [ow-toh-res-pee-ra-*toh*-ray]
» *TRAVEL TIP: the use of an aqualung for underwater fishing is forbidden in Italian waters*

archaeology l'archeologia [–*jee*-ah]
area area [*ah*-ray-ah]
arm il braccio [br*ah*-choh]
around *see* **about**
arrange: will you arrange it? ci pensa lei? [chee-pen-sah lay]
it's all arranged è tutto a posto [eh . . .]
arrest: he's been arrested è stato arrestato [eh st*ah*-toh . . .]
arrival l'arrivo [ar-r*ee*-voh]
arrive arrivare [ar-ree-v*ah*-ray]
we only arrived yesterday siamo arrivati solo ieri [. . . y*eh*-ree]
arrivi *arrivals*
art l'arte [*a*r-tay]
art gallery una galleria d'arte [gal-lay-r*ee*-ah . . .]
arthritis l'artrite [ar-tr*ee*-tay]
artificial artificiale [ar-tee-fee-ch*ah*-lay]
artist l'artista
as: as quickly as you can il più in fretta possibile [eel pew een fr*ay*t-tah pos-s*ee*-bee-lay]
as much as you can il più che può [. . . kay pwoh]
do as I do faccia come me [f*ah*-chah k*oh*-may may]
as you like come le pare [k*oh*-may lay p*ah*-ray]
ascensore *lift*
ashore a terra
to go ashore sbarcare [sbar-k*ah*-ray]
we've run ashore siamo incagliati [. . . een-kal-y*ah*-tee]
ashtray un portacenere [por-ta-ch*ay*-nay-ray]
ask chiedere [kee-*ay*-day-ray]
could you ask him to do it for me? può chiedergli di farlo per me? [pwoh kee-*ay*-der-lee dee . . . may]
that's not what I asked for non è quello che

ho chiesto [. . . kay o kee-*es*-toh]
asleep: he's still asleep è ancora addormentato [eh . . .]
asparagus gli asparagi [lee as-p*ah*-ra-jee]
aspirin un'aspirina
assistant l'assistente [–tay]
shop assistant la commessa
asthma l'asma
at: at the café al caffè [kaf-f*eh*]
at my hotel al mio albergo
atmosphere l'atmosfera
attenti al cane *beware of the dog*
attenzione *caution*
attitude l'atteggiamento [at-tay-ja-m*e*n-toh]
attractive attraente [at-tra-*e*n-tay]
I think you're very attractive ti [tee] trovo molto attraente
aubergine la melanzana [may-lan-tz*ah*-nah]
August agosto
aunt la zia [tz*ee*-ah]
Australia l'Australia [ows-tr*a*l-yah]
Australian australiano [ows-tral-y*ah*-noh]
Austria l'Austria [*ow*s-tree-ah]
Austrian austriaco [ows-tr*ee*-a-koh]
authorities le autorità [ow-toh-ree-t*ah*]
automatic *(car)* un'automatica [ow-toh-m*ah*-tee-kah]
autostrada *motorway*
autumn l'autunno [ow-t*oo*n-noh]
in the autumn in autunno
avanti *cross now*
away: is it far away from here? è molto lontano da qua? [eh . . .]
go away! va' via! [. . . v*ee*-ah]
awful terribile [ter-r*ee*-bee-lay]
axle l'asse [*a*s-say]
baby il bamb*i*no
we'd like a baby-sitter vorremmo una baby-sitter

back: I've got a bad back ho il mal di schiena [o eel mal dee skee-*ay*-nah]
I'll be back soon torno subito [. . . *soo*-bee-toh]
is he back? è tornato? [eh . . .]
can I have my money back? posso avere indietro il denaro? [. . . a-*vay*-ray een-dee-*eh*-troh . . .]
come back torni indietro
I go back tomorrow ritorno domani
at the back dietro [dee-*eh*-troh]
bacon la pancetta affumicata [pan-ch*ay*t-tah . . .]
bacon and eggs pancetta e uova [. . . ay w*o*-vah]
bad cattivo [kat-*tee*-voh]
it's not bad non c'è male [non cheh m*ah*-lay]
too bad! pazienza! [pa-tzee-*e*n-tzah]
bag una borsa; *(handbag)* una borsetta
baggage i bagagli [ee ba-g*a*l-yee]
bagno *bathroom*
baker's il panettiere [pa-nayt-y*eh*-ray]
balcony il balcone [bal-k*oh*-nay]
a room with a balcony una *ca*mera con balcone
ball una palla
ball-point pen una biro [*bee*-roh]
banana una banana
band *(music)* l'orche*s*tra
bandage una benda
could you change the bandage? può cambiare la benda? [pwoh kam-bee-*ah*-ray . . .]
bank la banca *(river)* la sponda
» *TRAVEL TIP: banks in Italy are open from 8.30 to 1.30; 'bank holidays' see* **'public holidays'**
bar il bar
when does the bar open? quando apre il bar? [. . . *ah*-pray . . .]
» *TRAVEL TIP: in most bars you must pay at the cash*

desk before ordering and show your ticket (scontrino) at the bar
YOU MAY HEAR . . .
ritiri lo scontrino alla cassa *get your ticket at the cash desk*
barber il barbiere [bar-bee-*ay*-ray]
bargain: it's a real bargain è proprio un affare [. . . af-*fah*-ray]
barman il barista [ba-*ree*s-tah]
basket il cestino [ches-*tee*-noh]
bath il bagno [*ba*n-yoh]
can I have a bath? posso fare [*fah*-ray] il bagno?
could you give me a bath towel? può darmi un asciugamano da bagno? [pwoh *da*r-mee oon a-shoo-ga-m*ah*-noh dah . . .]
bathing costume un costume da bagno [kos-*too*-may . . .]
bathroom il bagno [*ba*n-yoh]
we want a room with a private bathroom vorremmo una camera con bagno
can I use your bathroom? posso usare [oo-*zah*-ray] il bagno?
battery una pila [*pee*-lah] *(car)* la batteria [bat-tay-*ree*-ah]
be essere [*e*s-say-ray]
be . . . sia . . .
don't be . . . non sia . . .
beach la spiaggia [spee-*ah*-jah]
see you on the beach ci [chee] vediamo in spiaggia
beans i fagioli [ee fa-j*oh*-lee]
beautiful bello
a beautiful woman una bella donna
that was a beautiful meal il pranzo era molto buono [eel *pra*n-tzoh *eh*-rah *mo*l-toh bw*o*-noh]
because perché [per-k*ay*]
because of the weather a causa del tempo [ah k*ow*-zah . . .]

bed il letto
single bed/double bed letto singolo/letto matrimoniale [. . .–ah-lay]
you haven't changed my bed non avete cambiato le lenzuola [non a-v*ay*-tay kam-bee-*ah*-toh lay layn-tzw*o*-lah]
I want to go to bed voglio andare a dormire [v*o*l-yoh an-d*ah*-ray ah dor-m*ee*-ray]
bed and breakfast una pensione [payn-see-*oh*-nay]
bee un'ape [*ah*-pay]
beef il manzo [m*a*n-tzoh]
beer la birra [b*ee*r-rah]
two beers, please due birre, per favore [d*oo*-ay b*ee*r-ray payr fa-v*oh*-ray]
before: before breakfast prima di colazione [pr*ee*-mah dee ko-la-tzee-*oh*-nay]
before we leave prima di partire [. . . –ray]
I haven't been here before non c'ero mai stato [non ch*eh*-roh m*ah*-ee . . .]
begin: when does it begin? quando inizia? [kw*a*n-doh ee-n*ee*-tzee-ah]
I'm a beginner sono un principiante [. . . preen-chee-pee-*a*n-tay]
behind dietro [dee-*eh*-troh]
the car behind me l'auto dietro [ow-toh . . .]
believe: I don't believe you non la credo [. . . kr*ay*-doh]
I believe you la credo
bell *(in hotel etc)* il campanello
belong: that belongs to me mi appartiene [mee ap-par-tee-*ay*-nay]
who does this belong to? a chi appartiene? [ah kee . . .]
below sotto
belt la cintura [cheen-t*oo*-rah]
bend *(in road)* una curva [k*oo*r-vah]
berries le bacche [b*a*k-kay]
berth *(on ship)* una cuccetta [koo-ch*ay*t-tah]

beside accanto a
best migliore [meel-*yoh*-ray]
it's the best holiday I've ever had è la migliore vacanza che abbia fatto [. . . va-*kan*-tzah kay . . .]
better meglio [m*e*l-yoh]
haven't you got anything better? non ha niente di meglio? [non ah nee-*e*n-tay dee . . .]
are you feeling better? si sente meglio? [see s*e*n-tay . . .]
I'm feeling a lot better mi [mee] sento molto meglio
between tra
beyond oltre [*o*l-tray]
bicycle la bicicletta [bee-chee-kl*ay*t-tah]
big grande [–day]
a big one uno grande
that's too big è troppo grande [eh . . .]
it's not big enough non è grande abbastanza [. . . ab-bas-*ta*n-tzah]
have you got a bigger one? ne avete uno più grande? [nay a-v*ay*-tay *oo*-noh pew . . .]
biglietti *tickets*
bikini il bikini
bill il conto
could I have the bill, please? potrei avere il conto? [po-tr*ay* a-v*ay*-ray . . .]
» *TRAVEL TIP: service – see* **tipping**
binario *platform*
binding *(skiing)* l'attacco
bird un uccello [oo-ch*e*l-loh]
birthday il compleanno [kom-play-*a*n-noh]
it's my birthday è il mio compleanno [eh eel m*ee*-oh . . .]
happy birthday buon compleanno [bwon . . .]
biscuit un biscotto
bit: just a bit solo un po'
a bit of that cake un pezzo di quella torta [p*e*t-tzoh dee . . .]

that's a bit too expensive è un po' troppo caro
a big bit un bel pezzo
bite *(noun)* un morso
I've been bitten sono stato punto [. . . st*ah*-toh p*oo*n-toh] *(by dog)* sono stato morso
bitter *(taste)* amaro
black nero [n*ay*-roh]
he's had a blackout è svenuto
bland blando
blanket una coperta
I'd like another blanket vorrei un'altra coperta [vor-ray . . .]
bleach la candeggina [kan-day-j*ee*-nah]
bleed sanguinare [san-gwee-n*ah*-ray]
he's bleeding sanguina
bless you *(after sneeze)* salute! [–tay]
blind cieco [ch*eh*-koh]
blind spot *(driving)* zona cieca [tz*o*-nah . . .]
blister una vescica [vay-sh*ee*-kah]
blocked bloccato
blonde una bionda [bee-*o*n-dah]
blood il sangue [s*a*n-gway]
his blood group is . . . il suo gruppo sanguigno è . . . [. . . gr*oo*p-poh san-gw*ee*n-yoh . . .]
I've got high blood pressure ho la pressione alta [o lah prays-y*oh*-nay . . .]
he needs a blood transfusion ha bisogno di una trasfusione [ah bee-s*o*nn-yoh dee . . . –nay]
bloody mary un bloody mary
blouse una camicetta [ka-mee-ch*ay*t-tah]
blue blu
board: full board la pensione completa [pen-see-*oh*-nay . . .]
half board la mezza pensione [m*e*t-tzah . . .]
boarding pass la carta d'imbarco
boat una barca

boat train treno di coincidenza con la nave [. . . dee ko-een-chee-*den*-tzah kon lah *nah*-vay]
body il corpo *(dead body)* un morto
boil *(verb)* bollire [–ray]
(noun) una pustola [*poo*s-toh-lah]
do we have to boil the water? dobbiamo bollire l'acqua?
boiled egg un uovo alla coque [*wo*-voh *a*l-lah kok]
bone un osso
bonnet *(car)* il cofano [*ko*-fa-noh]
book un libro [*lee*-broh]
booking office l'ufficio prenotazioni [oof-*fee*-choh pray-no-ta-tzee-*oh*-nee]
can I book a ticket to . . ./for . . . posso prenotare un biglietto per . . . [. . . beel-*ye*t-toh . . .]
I'd like to book a table for two vorrei prenotare un tavolo per due [vor-*ray* pray-no-*tah*-ray oon *tah*-vo-lo payr *doo*-ay]
bookshop una libreria [–*ee*-ah]
boot *(shoe)* uno stivale [stee-*vah*-lay]
(car) il portabagagli [por-ta-ba-*ga*l-yee]
booze: I had too much booze ho [o] bevuto troppo
border il confine [kon-*fee*-nay]
bored: I'm bored sono annoiato [an-no-*yah*-toh]
boring noioso [no-*yoh*-soh]
born: I was born in 1956 sono nato nel millenovecentocinquantasei [. . . m*ee*l-lay-no-vay-*che*n-toh-cheen-kwan-ta-*say*]
borrow: can I borrow . . .? posso avere in prestito . . .? [. . . a-*vay*-ray een pr*e*s-tee-toh]
boss il capo
both entrambi [en-*tra*m-bee]
I'll take both of them li prendo entrambi [lee . . .]
bottle una bottiglia [bot-*tee*l-yah]

bottle-opener un apribottiglia
bottom: at the bottom of the hill in fondo alla collina
bouncer il buttafuori [boot-tah-fw*o*-ree]
bowels l'intestino [een-tes-*tee*-noh]
bowl una scodella
box una scatola [sk*ah*-toh-lah]
boy il ragazzo [ra-g*a*t-tzoh]
boyfriend: my boyfriend il mio ragazzo [m*ee*-oh ra-g*a*t-tzoh]; *(older)* il mio amico
bra il reggiseno [reh-jee-s*ay*-noh]
bracelet il braccialetto [bra-cha-l*ay*t-toh]
brake *(noun)* il freno [fr*ay*-noh]
could you check the brakes? può controllare i freni? [pwoh kon-trol-l*ah*-ray ee . . .]
I had to brake suddenly ho dovuto frenare all'improvviso [o do-v*oo*-toh fray-n*ah*-ray . . . –v*ee*-soh]
he didn't brake non ha [ah] frenato
brandy un brandy
bread il pane [p*ah*-nay]
could we have some bread and butter? potremmo avere del pane e burro? [. . . a-v*ay*-ray . . .]
some more bread, please ancora del pane, per favore [. . . fa-v*oh*-ray]
break *(verb)* rompere [r*o*m-pay-ray]
I think I've broken my arm penso d'aver rotto il braccio [. . . br*ah*-choh]
breakable fragile [fr*ah*-jee-lay]
breakdown un guasto [gw*a*s-toh]
I've had a breakdown ho avuto un guasto [o . . .]
nervous breakdown l'esaurimento nervoso [ay-zow-ree-m*e*n-toh . . .]
» *TRAVEL TIP: breakdown services – phone 116*
breakfast la colazione [ko-la-tzee-*oh*-nay]
breast il petto
breath il fiato [fee-*ah*-toh]

breathe respirare [res-pee-*rah*-ray]
I can't breathe non posso respirare
bridge il ponte [*po*n-tay]
briefcase la valigetta [va-lee-*jay*t-tal.]
brighten up: do you think it'll brighten up later? pensa che si rischiarerà più tardi? [. . . kay see rees-kee-a-ray-*rah* pew *ta*r-dee]
brilliant *(very good)* brillante [–tay]
bring portare [por-*tah*-ray]
could you bring it to my hotel? può [pwoh] portarlo al mio albergo?
Britain la Gran Bretagna [. . . bray-*ta*n-yah]
British inglese [een-*glay*-say]
brochure un opuscolo [o-*poo*s-ko-loh]
have you got any brochures about . . .? ha un opuscolo su . . .? [ah . . .]
broken rotto
you've broken it l'ha rotto [lah . . .]
it's broken è rotto [eh . . .]
my room/car has been broken into mi hanno svaligiato la camera/l'auto [mee *a*n-noh sva-lee-*jah*-toh la *kah*-may-rah/*low*-toh]
brooch una spilla [*spee*l-lah]
brother: my brother mio fratello [m*ee*-oh . . .]
brown marrone [mar-*roh*-nay]
brown paper la carta da pacchi [. . . *pa*k-kee]
browse: can I just browse around? posso curiosare? [. . . –*sah*-ray]
bruise una ammaccatura
brunette una mora
brush *(noun)* una spazzola [*spa*t-tzo-lah]
(artist's) un pennello
Brussels sprouts i cavolini di Bruxelles [. . . dee brook-*se*l]
bucket il secchio [*say*k-yoh]
buffet il buffet
building un edificio [ay-dee-*fee*-choh]
bulb: the bulb's gone la lampadina è rotta [lam-pa-*dee*-nah eh . . .]

bump: he's had a bump on the head ha urtato la testa [ah . . .]
bumper il paraurti [pa-ra-*oo*r-tee]
bunch of flowers un mazzo di fiori [m*a*t-tzoh dee fee-*oh*-ree]
bunk una cuccetta [koo-ch*ay*t-tah]
bunk beds i letti a castello
buoy una boa
burglar un ladro
they've taken all my money mi hanno rubato tutto il denaro [mee *a*n-noh . . .]
burnt: this meat is burnt questa carne è bruciata [. . . k*a*r-nay eh broo-ch*ah*-tah]
my arms are burnt mi sono scottato le braccia [. . . br*ah*-chah]
can you give me something for these burns? mi può dare qualcosa per queste scottature? [mee pwoh d*ah*-ray . . . skot-ta-t*oo*-ray]
bus l'autobus [*ow*-toh-boos]
bus stop la fermata dell'autobus
could you tell me when we get there? me lo può dire quando ci siamo? [may loh pwoh d*ee*-ray kw*a*n-doh chee see-*ah*-moh]
» *TRAVEL TIP: get tickets from machine on the bus; or buy a book of tickets from news-stand or tobacconist; usually flat fare; in Rome and Milan underground tickets valid for bus travel up to 1 hour from issue*
business: I'm here on business sono qui per affari [. . . kwee payr . . .]
business trip un viaggio d'affari [vee-*ah*-joh . . .]
none of your business non è affar suo [. . . eh . . .]
bust il busto [b*oo*s-toh]
» *TRAVEL TIP: bust measurements*

UK	*32*	*34*	*36*	*38*	*40*
Italy	*80*	*87*	*91*	*97*	*102*

busy occupato

but ma
not this one but that one non questo ma quello
butcher il macellaio [ma-chel-l*ah*-yoh]
butter il burro [b*oo*r-roh]
button un bottone [bot-t*oh*-nay]
buy: where can I buy . . .? dove posso comprare [d*oh*-vay . . . kom-pr*ah*-ray]
I'll buy it lo compro
by: I'm here by myself sono qui [kwee] da solo
are you by yourself? è qui da solo? [eh . . .]
can you do it by tomorrow? può farlo per domani? [pwoh . . . payr . . .]
by train/car/plane in treno/auto/aereo [een tr*eh*-noh/*ow*-toh/ah-*eh*-ray-oh]
I parked by the trees ho parcheggiato vicino agli alberi [o par-kay-j*ah*-toh vee-ch*ee*-noh *a*l-yee *a*l-bay-ree]
who's it made by? chi l'ha fatto? [kee lah . . .]
c *(on tap) hot*
cabaret il cabaret
cabbage un cavolo [k*ah*-vo-loh]
cable il cavo [k*ah*-voh]
cable car la funivia [–v*ee*-ah]
cabin *(on ship)* una cabina
caduta massi *falling rocks*
cafe un caffè [kaf-f*eh*]
» TRAVEL TIP: *Italian cafes also serve alcoholic drinks, but only snacks – toasted sandwiches and cakes; for cafe-type food look for the sign 'tavola calda'*
cake una pasta
a piece of cake un pezzo di torta [p*e*t-tzoh dee . . .]
calculator un calcolatore [–t*oh*-ray]
call: will you call the manager? mi chiama il direttore? [mee kee-*ah*-mah eel dee-rayt-t*oh*-ray]
what is this called? come si [see] chiama?

call box un telefono pubblico [tay-*leh*-fo-noh *poo*b-blee-koh]
calm calmo
calm down si calmi [see . . .]
camera la macchina fotografica [*ma*k-kee-nah . . .]
camp: is there somewhere we can camp? dove possiamo accamparci? [d*oh*-vay . . . ak-kam-*pa*r-chee]
can we camp here? possiamo accamparci qua?
camping holiday una vacanza campeggio [va-*ka*n-tzah kam-*pay*-joh]
campsite un camping
» *TRAVEL TIP: in Italy you can camp almost anywhere; the best campsites are those recommended by ENIT (the national tourist organization)*
can¹: a can of beer una lattina di birra [. . . dee *bee*r-rah]
can-opener un apriscatole [a-pree-sk*ah*-toh-lay]
can²: can I have . . .? posso avere . . .? [. . . a-*vay*-ray]
can you show me . . .? può mostrarmi [pwoh . . . –mee]
I can't . . . non posso . . .
he can't . . . non può . . .
can we . . .? possiamo . . .?
Canada il Canada
Canadian canadese [ka-na-*day*-say]
cancel: I want to cancel my booking vorrei cancellare la mia prenotazione [vor-*ray* kan-chel-*lah*-ray lah m*ee*-ah pray-no-ta-tzee-*oh*-nay]
can we cancel dinner for tonight? possiamo cancellare la cena per stasera? [. . . ch*ay*-nah . . . sta-*say*-rah]
candle una candela [–*day*-lah]

by candlelight al lume di candela [*loo*-may dee . . .]
capsize capovolgersi [ka-po-*vol*-jer-see]
car l'auto [*ow*-toh], la macchina [*mak*-kee-nah]
by car in macchina
carafe una caraffa
caravan la roulotte [–lot]
carburettor il carburatore [–*toh*-ray]
cards le carte [*kar*-tay]
do you play cards? gioca a carte? [*jo*-kah . . .]
care: will you take care of this for me? può prendersi cura di questo per me? [pwoh *pren*-der-see *koo*-rah dee *kwes*-toh payr may]
careful: be careful sta attento
car-ferry il traghetto [tra-*ghet*-toh]
car park un parcheggio [par-*kay*-joh]
carpet il tappeto *(wall-to-wall)* la moquette [–*ket*]
carrot la carota
carry: will you carry this for me? mi può portare questo? [mee pwoh por-*tah*-ray . . .]
carry-cot la culla portatile [*kool*-lah por-ta-*tee*-lay]
carving un intaglio [een-*tal*-yoh]
case *(suitcase)* una valigia [va-*lee*-jah]
casello a . . . *motorway toll at . . .*
cash *(money)* soldi [*sol*-dee]
I haven't any cash non l'ho di moneta [. . . lo dee mo-*nay*-tah]
cash desk la cassa
will you cash a cheque for me? può riscuotere un assegno per me? [pwoh rees-*kwoh*-tay-ray oon as-*sayn*-yoh payr may]
casino il casinò [ka-see-*noh*]
» *TRAVEL TIP: it is important to stress the last syllable; pronounced as in English the word means brothel*
cassa *cash point; cashier*
cassette una cassetta

castle il castello
cat il gatto
catch: where do we catch the bus? dove si prende l'autobus? [d*oh*-vay see pr*e*n-day l*ow*-toh-boos]
he's caught a bug si è preso un malanno [see eh pr*ay*-soh . . .]
cathedral la cattedrale [–dr*ah*-lay]
catholic cattolico [kat-t*oh*-lee-koh]
cauliflower il cavolfiore [–*oh*-ray]
cave la grotta
ceiling il soffitto
celery il sedano [s*eh*-da-noh]
cellophane il cellophane [ch*e*l-lo-fa-nay]
centigrade centigradi [chen-t*ee*-gra-dee]
» TRAVEL TIP: *to convert C to F:* $\frac{C}{5} \times 9 + 32 = F$

centigrade	*−5*	*0*	*10*	*15*	*21*	*30*	*36.9*
Fahrenheit	*23*	*32*	*50*	*59*	*70*	*86*	*98.4*

centimetre un centimetro [chen-t*ee*-may-troh]
» TRAVEL TIP: *1 cm = 0.39 inches*
central centrale [chen-tr*ah*-lay]
with central heating con riscaldamento centrale
centre il centro [ch*e*n-troh]
how do we get to the centre? come si va in centro? [k*oh*-may see . . .]
certain certo [ch*ay*r-toh]
are you certain? è certo? [eh . . .]
certificate il certificato [cher-tee-fee-k*ah*-toh]
chain la catena [ka-t*ay*-nah]
chair la sedia [s*eh*-dee-ah]
chairlift la seggiovia [seh-jo-v*ee*-ah]
chambermaid la cameriera [ka-may-ree-*eh*-rah]
champagne lo champagne [shom-p*a*n-yuh]
change: could you change this into lire? può cambiare questi in lire? [pwoh kam-bee-*ah*-ray . . .]

I haven't any change non ho moneta [. . . o mo-*nay*-tah]
do we have to change trains? dobbiamo cambiare treno?
I'll just get changed vado a cambiarmi
» TRAVEL TIP: *don't be surprised if instead of small change you get chewing gum or sweets when shopping or in a bar!*
» TRAVEL TIP: *changing money: as well as banks look for 'Agenzia di Cambio'*
channel: the Channel la Manica [*mah*-nee-kah]
charge: what do you charge? quanto fate pagare? [. . . *fah*-tay pa-*gah*-ray]
who's in charge? chi è l'incaricato? [kee eh . . .]
chart la carta
cheap a buon mercato [ah bwon mayr-*kah*-toh]
something cheaper qualcosa di meno caro [. . . dee *may*-noh . . .]
cheat: I've been cheated sono stato imbrogliato [. . . *stah*-toh eem-brol-*yah*-toh]
check: will you check? può controllare? [pwoh . . . –*ah*-ray]
I'm sure, I've checked sono sicuro, ho controllato [. . . o . . .]
will you check the total? può controllare il totale [. . . –lay]
we checked in ci siamo registrati [chee . . .]
we checked out abbiamo pagato il conto
cheek la guancia [*gwa*n-chah]
cheeky sfacciato [sfa-*chah*-toh]
cheerio ciao [chow]
(toast) cin cin [cheen cheen]
cheers salute [–tay] *(thank you)* grazie [*grah*-tzee-ay]
cheese il formaggio [for-*mah*-joh]
chef lo chef
chemist's la farmacia [far-ma-*chee*-ah]

cheque un assegno [as-*say*n-yoh]
will you take a cheque? prende un assegno? [pr*e*n-day . . .]
cheque book il libretto di assegni [. . . dee . . .]
cheque card il cheque card
chest il petto [p*e*t-toh]
» *TRAVEL TIP: chest measurements*

UK	*34*	*36*	*38*	*40*	*42*	*44*	*46*
Italy	*87*	*91*	*97*	*102*	*107*	*112*	*117*

chewing gum la gomma da masticare [–k*ah*-ray]
chicken il pollo
chickenpox la varicella [va-ree-ch*e*l-lah]
child il bambino [bam-b*ee*-noh]
children i bambini [ee bam-b*ee*-nee]
children's portion una porzione per bambini [. . . por-tzee-*oh*-nay . . .]
chin il mento
china la porcellana [por-chel-l*ah*-nah]
chips le patatine fritte [lay pa-ta-t*ee*-nay fr*ee*t-tay]
(casino) le fiches [lay feesh]
chiuso *closed*
chocolate il cioccolato [chok-ko-l*ah*-toh]
hot chocolate la cioccolata calda
a box of chocolates una scatola di cioccolatini [sk*ah*-toh-lah dee . . .]
choke *(car)* la valvola dell'aria [v*a*l-vo-lah del-l*ah*-ree-ah]
chop *(noun)* una cotoletta
Christmas Natale [na-t*ah*-lay]
happy Christmas! buon Natale! [bwon . . .]
church la chiesa [kee-*ay*-sah]
where is the Protestant/Catholic church? dov'è la chiesa protestante/cattolica? [doh-v*eh* . . . pro-tes-t*a*n-tay/kat-t*oh*-lee-kah]
cider il sidro [s*ee*-droh]
cigar il sigaro [s*ee*-ga-roh]

cigarette una sigaretta
would you like a cigarette? vuole una sigaretta? [vw*oh*-lay . . .]
cine-camera la cinepresa [chee-nay-pr*ay*-sah]
cinema il cinema [ch*ee*-nay-mah]
circle il circolo [ch*ee*r-ko-loh]
(in cinema) la galleria [–*ee*-ah]
city la città [cheet-t*ah*]
claim *(noun: insurance)* la domanda d'indennizzo [. . . deen-den-n*ee*t-tzoh]
clarify chiarire [kee-a-r*ee*-ray]
clean *(adjective)* pulito [poo-l*ee*-toh]
can I have some clean sheets? posso avere le lenzuola pulite? [. . . a-v*ay*-ray lay layn-tzw*o*-lah . . .]
my room hasn't been cleaned today la mia stanza non è stata pulita oggi [m*ee*-ah st*a*n-tzah . . . eh . . . *o*-jee]
it's not clean non è pulito
cleansing cream il detergente [–tay]
clear: I'm not clear about it non è chiaro [. . . eh kee-*ah*-roh]
clever intelligente [–tay]
climate il clima [kl*ee*-mah]
climb: we're going to climb . . . andiamo a scalare . . . [. . . ska-l*ah*-ray]
climber uno scalatore [–t*oh*-ray]
clip *(skiing)* la pinzetta [peen-tz*ay*t-tah]
cloakroom il guardaroba [gwar-da-r*o*-bah]
(WC) il gabinetto
clock l'orologio [–*oh*-joh]
close[1] vicino [vee-ch*ee*-noh]
(weather) afoso
close[2]**: when do you close?** quando chiudete? [. . . kee-oo-d*ay*-tay]
closed chiuso [kee-*oo*-soh]
cloth la stoffa *(rag)* uno straccio [str*ah*-choh]
clothes i vestiti [ee ves-t*ee*-tee]
cloud la nuvola [n*oo*-vo-lah]

clutch la frizione [free-tzee-*oh*-nay]
the clutch is slipping la frizione non si [see] innesta
coach la corriera [kor-*yeh*-rah]
coast la costa
coastguard la guardia costiera [gw*a*r-dee-ah kos-tee-*eh*-rah]
coat il cappotto
cockroach uno scarafaggio [–f*a*dj-yoh]
coffee un caffè [kaf-f*eh*]
white coffee un cappuccino [kap-poo-ch*ee*-noh]
» *TRAVEL TIP: in Italy coffee is always served black and very strong; if you want it less strong ask for 'un caffé lungo'*
coin una moneta [mo-n*ay*-tah]
cold *(adjective)* freddo
I'm cold ho freddo [o . . .]
I've got a cold ho il raffreddore [. . . –d*oh*-ray]
collapse: he's collapsed ha avuto un collasso [ah . . .]
collar il colletto
collarbone l'osso del collo
» *TRAVEL TIP: collar sizes*

(old) UK	*14*	*14½*	*15*	*15½*	*16*	*16½*	*17*
continental	*36*	*37*	*38*	*39*	*41*	*42*	*43*

collect: I want to collect . . . sono venuto a prendere . . . [. . . pr*e*n-day-ray]
colour un colore [ko-l*oh*-ray]
have you any other colours? avete altri colori? [a-v*ay*-tay . . .]
comb il pettine [p*e*t-tee-nay]
come venire [vay-n*ee*-ray]
I come from London sono di [dee] Londra
we came here yesterday siamo arrivati ieri [. . . *yeh*-ree]
come on! andiamo!
come with me venga con me [. . . may]
come here venga qui [. . . kwee]

comfortable comodo [k*o*-mo-doh]
it's not very comfortable non è molto comodo
Common Market il Mercato Comune [mayr-*kah*-toh ko-m*oo*-nay]
communication cord il segnale d'allarme [sayn-*yah*-lay dal-l*a*r-may]
company la compagnia [kom-pan-*yee*-ah]
you're good company sei simpatico [say seem-p*ah*-tee-koh]
compartment *(train)* uno scompartimento
compass la bussola [b*oo*s-so-lah]
compensation un compenso
I demand compensation voglio un compenso [v*o*l-yoh . . .]
complaint una lamentela
I want to complain about my room vorrei sporgere una lamentela a proposito della mia stanza [vor-*ray* sp*o*r-jay-ray . . . m*ee*-ah st*a*n-tzah]
completely completamente [–m*ay*n-tay]
complicated: it's very complicated è molto complicato [eh . . .]
compliment: my compliments to the chef i miei complimenti allo chef [ee mee-*eh*-ee . . .]
concert un concerto [kon-ch*ay*r-toh]
concussion la commozione cerebrale [. . . –tzee-*oh*-nay chay-ray-br*ah*-lay]
condition la condizione [–tzee-*oh*-nay]
it's not in very good condition non è in buone condizioni [. . . eh een bw*o*-nay . . .]
conference una conferenza [–*e*n-tzah]
confirm confermare [kon-fayr-m*ah*-ray]
confuse: you're confusing me mi confonde [mee kon-f*o*n-day]
congratulations! complimenti! [–tee]
conjunctivitis la congiuntivite [kon-joon-tee-v*ee*-tay]
connection *(rail etc)* la coincidenza [ko-een-chee-d*e*n-tzah]

connoisseur un conoscitore [ko-no-shee-*toh*-ray]
conscious conscio [*ko*n-shoh]
consciousness: he's lost consciousness è svenuto [eh . . .]
constipation la stitichezza [stee-tee-k*ay*t-tzah]
consul il console [*ko*n-so-lay]
consulate il consolato
contact: how can I contact . . .? come mi metto in contatto con . . .? [k*oh*-may mee . . .]
 contact lenses le lenti a contatto
contraceptive un contraccettivo [kon-tra-chet-*tee*-voh]
convenient conveniente [–en-tay]
cook: it's not cooked è crudo
 it's beautifully cooked è cucinato alla perfezione [eh koo-chee-n*ah*-toh *a*l-lah per-fay-tzee-*oh*-nay]
 cooker la cucina [koo-ch*ee*-nah]
cool fresco
corkscrew un cavatappi
corn *(foot)* un callo
corner un angolo [*a*n-go-loh]
 can we have a corner table? possiamo avere un tavolo d'angolo [. . . a-v*ay*-ray oon t*ah*-vo-loh . . .]
cornflakes i [ee] corn flakes
correct corretto
cosmetics i cosmetici [ee kos-m*eh*-tee-chee]
cost: what does it cost? quanto costa?
 that's too much è troppo
 I'll take it lo compro
cotton il cotone [ko-t*oh*-nay]
 cotton wool il cotone idrofilo [. . . ee-dr*o*-fee-loh]
couchette la poltrona
cough la tosse [t*o*s-say]
 cough drops le pastiglie per la tosse [pas-t*ee*l-yay . . .]

could: could you please . . .? potrebbe . . .? [po-t*ray*b-bay]
could I have . . .? potrei avere? [po-t*ray* a-v*ay*-ray]
country un paese [pa-*ay*-say]
in the country in campagna [een kam-p*a*n-yah]
couple: a couple of . . . un paio di . . . [p*ah*-yoh dee]
courier la guida [gw*ee*-dah]
course *(of meal)* una portata
of course certo [ch*ay*r-toh]
court: I'll take you to court la cito in tribunale [lah ch*ee*-toh een tree-boo-n*ah*-lay]
cousin un cugino [koo-j*ee*-noh]
cover: keep him well covered lo tenga ben coperto; **cover charge** il coperto
cow la mucca [m*oo*k-kah]
crab il granchio [gr*a*n-kee-oh]
crash: there's been a crash c'è stato uno scontro [cheh st*ah*-toh . . .]
crash helmet un casco
crazy: you're crazy è pazzo [eh p*a*t-tzoh]
cream la crema *(fresh)* la panna
creche l'asilo nido [a-s*ee*-loh n*ee*-doh]
credit card una carta di credito [. . . dee kr*eh*-dee-toh]
crisis una crisi [kr*ee*-see]
crisps le patatine [pa-ta-t*ee*-nay]
crossroads l'incrocio [een-kr*oh*-choh]
crowded affollato
cruise una crociera [kro-ch*ay*-rah]
crutch una gruccia [gr*oo*-chah]
(of body) l'inguine [*ee*n-gwee-nay]
cry: don't cry non piangere [non pee-*a*n-jay-ray]
cup una tazza [t*a*t-tzah]
a cup of coffee una tazza di caffè [. . . dee kaf-f*eh*]

cupboard un armadio [ar-*mah*-dee-oh]
curry il curry
curtains le tende [*ten*-day]
cushion il cuscino [koo-*shee*-noh]
Customs la Dogana
cut: I've cut myself mi sono tagliato [mee-*soh*-noh tal-*yah*-toh]
cycle: can we cycle there? ci si può andare con la bicicletta? [chee see pwoh an-*dah*-ray kon la bee-chee-*klayt*-tah]
cyclist un ciclista [chee-*klees*-tah]
cylinder il cilindro [chee-*leen*-droh]
  cylinder head gasket la guarnizione del cilindro [gwar-nee-tzee-*oh*-nay . . .]
dad(dy) il papà
damage: I'll pay for the damage pago per il guasto [*gwas*-toh]
  it's damaged è danneggiato [eh dan-nay-*jah*-toh]
damn! maledizione! [ma-lay-dee-tzee-*oh*-nay]
damp umido [*oo*-mee-doh]
dance: is there a dance on? si balla? [see . . .]
  would you like to dance? vuoi ballare? [vw*o*-ee bal-*lah*-ray]
dangerous pericoloso
dark scuro
  when does it get dark? quando fa buio? [. . . *boo*-yoh]
  dark green verde scuro [*vayr*-day . . .]
darling tesoro
dashboard il cruscotto
date: what's the date? quanti ne [nay] abbiamo?
  can we fix a date? possiamo fissare un appuntamento? [. . . fees-*sah*-ray . . .]
  on the first of March il primo marzo [*pree*-moh *mar*-tzoh]
  on the fifth of May il cinque maggio [*cheen*-kway *mah*-joh]

in 1982 nel millenovecentottantadue [mee*l*-lay-no-vay-che*n*-toh-ot-tan-ta-d*oo*-ay]
» *TRAVEL TIP: to say the date just use the ordinary number as shown above (the exception is 'the first'); numbers are listed on page 128*
dates *(fruit)* i datteri [ee d*a*t-tay-ree]
daughter: my daughter mia figlia [m*ee*-ah f*ee*l-yah]
day il giorno [j*o*r-noh]
dazzle: his lights were dazzling me i suoi fari mi abbagliavano [ee sw*oy*-ee f*ah*-ree mee ab-bal-y*ah*-va-noh]
dead morto
deaf sordo
deal *(business)* un affare [af-f*ah*-ray]
it's a deal affare fatto
will you deal with it? se ne occupa lei? [say nay *o*k-koo-pah lay]
dear *(expensive)* caro
Dear Sir Egregio Signore [ay-gr*ay*-joh seen-y*oh*-ray]
Dear Madam Egregia Signora
Dear Franco Caro Franco
December dicembre [dee-ch*e*m-bray]
deck il ponte [p*o*n-tay]
deckchair una sedia a sdraio [s*eh*-dee-ah ah sdr*ah*-yoh]
declare: I have nothing to declare non ho niente da dichiarare [non o nee-*e*n-tay dah deek-ya-r*ah*-ray]
deep profondo
is it deep? è profondo? [eh . . .]
defendant l'accusato
de-icer l'antighiaccio [an-teeg-y*ah*-choh]
delay: the flight was delayed il volo ha avuto un ritardo [. . . ah a-v*oo*-toh . . .]
deliberately apposta
delicate *(person)* delicato
delicatessen una salumeria [–may-r*ee*-ah]

delicious delizioso [day-lee-tzee-*oh*-soh]
delivery: is there another mail delivery? c'è un'altra distribuzione di posta? [cheh . . . –tzee-*oh*-nay dee *pos*-tah]
de luxe di lusso [dee *loo*s-soh]
democratic democratico [day-mo-kr*ah*-tee-koh]
dent una ammaccatura
you've dented my car ha ammaccato la mia auto [ah . . . m*ee*-ah *ow*-toh]
dentist il dentista
YOU MAY HEAR . . .
apra bene *open wide*
si sciacqui *please rinse out*
dentures la dentiera [dent-y*ay*-rah]
deny: I deny it lo nego
deodorant il deodorante [–tay]
departure la partenza [par-t*e*n-tzah]
depend: it depends (on him) dipende (da lui) [dee-p*e*n-day dah l*oo*-ee]
deport deportare [–t*ah*-ray]
deposit un deposito [day-p*o*-see-toh]
do I have to leave a deposit? devo lasciare un deposito? [d*ay*-voh la-sh*ah*-ray . . .]
deposito bagagli *left luggage*
depressed depresso
depth la profondità [pro-fon-dee-t*ah*]
desperate: I'm desperate for a drink ho una sete terribile [o *oo*-nah s*ay*-tay ter-r*ee*-bee-lay]
dessert il dolce [d*o*l-chay]
destination la destinazione [–tzee-*oh*-nay]
detergent il detergente [–j*e*n-tay]
detour una deviazione [–tzee-*oh*-nay]
devalued svalutato
develop: could you develop these? può sviluppare questi? [pwoh svee-loop-p*ah*-ray . . .]
deviazione *diversion*
diabetic un diabetico [dee-a-b*eh*-tee-koh]
dialling code il prefisso

diamond un diamante [–tay]
diarrhoea la diarrea [dee-ar-*ray*-ah]
have you got something for diarrhoea? ha qualcosa per la diarrea? [ah . . .]
diary il diario [dee-*ah*-ree-oh]
dictionary il dizionario [dee-tzee-o-*nah*-ree-oh]
didn't *see* **not**
die morire [mo-*ree*-ray]
he's dying sta morendo
diesel *(fuel)* il diesel
diet la dieta [dee-*ay*-tah]
I'm on a diet sono a dieta
different: they are different sono diversi
can I have a different room? posso avere un'altra camera? [. . . a-*vay*-ray . . .]
is there a different route? c'è un'altra strada? [cheh . . .]
difficult difficile [deef-*fee*-chee-lay]
digestion la digestione [–*oh*-nay]
dinghy il dinghy
dining room la sala da pranzo [. . . *pran*-tzoh]
dinner la cena [*chay*-nah]
dinner jacket lo smoking
dipped headlights gli anabbaglianti [lee a-nab-bal-*yan*-tee]
direct *(adjective)* diretto [dee–]
does it go direct? ci va diretto? [chee . . .]
dirty sporco
disabled invalido [een-*vah*-lee-doh]
disappear sparire [spa-*ree*-ray]
it's just disappeared è sparito [eh . . .]
disappointing deludente [–tay]
disco la discoteca
see you in the disco ci vediamo in discoteca [chee . . .]
discount lo sconto
disgusting disgustoso
dish un piatto [pee-*at*-toh]
dishonest disonesto

disinfectant un disinfettante [–tay], l'alcol
» *TRAVEL TIP: the latter, which is pure alcohol, usually pink in colour, is the standard disinfectant*
dispensing chemist la farmacia [far-ma-*chee*-ah]
distance: in the distance in lontananza [een lon-ta-*nan*-tzah]
distress signal un segnale di soccorso [sayn-*yah*-lay dee . . .]
distributor *(car)* lo spinterogeno [speen-tay-*ro*-jay-noh]
disturb: the noise is disturbing me il rumore mi disturba [eel roo-*moh*-ray mee dees-*too*r-bah]
divieto di . . . *do not . . .*
divorced divorziato [dee-vor-tzee-*ah*-toh]
do: how do you do? piacere [pee-a-*chay*-ray]
what are you doing tonight? cosa fa stasera?
how do you do it? come fa? [*koh*-may fah]
will you do it for me? lo può fare lei? [loh pwoh *fah*-ray lay]
I've never done it before non l'ho mai fatto prima [non lo *mah*-ee *fat*-toh *pree*-mah]
I was doing 60 kph andavo a sessanta all'ora
doctor il medico [*meh*-dee-koh]
I need a doctor ho bisogno di un medico [o bee-*so*nn-yoh dee . . .]
» *TRAVEL TIP: any chemist (farmacia) will have a list of the nearest doctors*
YOU MAY HEAR . . .
l'è mai successo prima? *have you had this before?*
dove le fa male? *where does it hurt?*
sta prendendo delle medicine? *are you taking any drugs?*
ne prenda una/due . . . *take one/two . . .*
una volta/due volte/tre volte al giorno *once/twice/three times a day*

document il documento
dog il cane [k*ah*-nay]
dogana *customs*
don't! no!; *see* **not**
door la porta
dosage la dose [d*oh*-say]
double: double room una camera a due letti [k*ah*-may-rah ah d*oo*-ay l*e*t-teeh]
(with double bed) una camera matrimoniale [–ee-*ah*-lay]
double whisky un whisky doppio [. . . d*o*p-pee-oh]
down: get down! giù! [joo]
downstairs dabbasso
it's just down the road è qui vicino [eh kwee vee-ch*ee*-noh]
drain il tubo di scarico [t*oo*-boh dee sk*ah*-ree-koh]
drawing pin una puntina [poon-t*ee*-nah]
dress un vestito [ves-t*ee*-toh]
dressing gown una vestaglia [ves-t*a*l-yah]

» *TRAVEL TIP: sizes*

UK	*10*	*12*	*14*	*16*	*18*	*20*
Italy	*38*	*40*	*42*	*44*	*46*	*48*

dressing *(for wound)* la medicazione [may-dee-ka-tzee-*oh*-nay]
(for salad) il condimento
drink: would you like something to drink? vuole bere qualcosa? [vw*oh*-lay b*ay*-ray . . .]
I don't drink non bevo alcolici [. . . b*ay*-voh al-k*oh*-lee-chee]
is the water drinkable? l'acqua è potabile? [. . . eh po-t*ah*-bee-lay]
drive guidare [gwee-d*ah*-ray]
I've been driving all day è tutto il giorno che guido [eh t*oo*t-toh eel j*o*r-noh kay . . .]
driver l'autista [low-t*ee*s-tah]
driving licence la patente [pa-t*e*n-tay]
drown: he's drowning sta annegando

drug la droga
drunk ubriaco [oo-bree-*ah*-koh]
dry *(adjective)* asciutto [a-sh*oo*t-toh]
(wine) secco
dry-cleaner's un lavasecco
due: when is the bus due? quando arriva l'autobus? [. . . l*ow*-toh-boos]
during durante [doo-r*a*n-tay]
dust la polvere [p*o*l-vay-ray]
duty-free *(noun)* il duty-free
dynamo la dinamo [d*ee*-na-moh]
each: can we have one each? possiamo averne uno ciascuno [. . . a-v*ay*r-nay *oo*-noh chas-k*oo*-noh]
how much are they each? quanto costano l'uno?
ear l'orecchio [or-r*ay*k-yoh]
I have earache ho il mal d'orecchi [o . . .]
early presto
we want to leave a day earlier vogliamo partire un giorno prima [vol-y*ah*-moh par-t*ee*-ray oon j*o*r-noh pr*ee*-mah]
early closing la chiusura anticipata [kee-oo-s*oo*-rah an-tee-chee-p*ah*-tah]
earring l'orecchino [o-rayk-k*ee*-noh]
east est
Easter Pasqua [p*a*s-kwah]
easy facile [f*ah*-chee-lay]
eat mangiare [man-j*ah*-ray]
something to eat qualcosa da mangiare
egg un uovo [w*o*-voh]
Eire l'Irlanda
either: either . . . or . . . o . . . o . . .
I don't like either non mi piace nessuno dei due [non mee pee-*ah*-chay nes-s*oo*-noh day d*oo*-ay]
elastic elastico [ay-l*a*s-tee-koh]
elastic band un elastico
elbow il gomito [g*o*-mee-toh]

electric elettrico [ay-*le*t-tree-koh]
electric blanket la coperta elettrica
electric fire la stufetta elettrica
electrician l'elettricista [ay-layt-tree-ch*ee*s-tah]
electricity l'elettricità [ay-layt-tree-chee-*tah*]
elegant elegante [. . .–tay]
else: something else qualcosa d'altro
somewhere else da qualche altra parte [dah-kw*a*l-kay *a*l-trah p*a*r-tay]
who else? chi altro? [kee . . .]
or else o altrimenti
embarrassed imbarazzato [eem-ba-rat-tz*ah*-toh]
embarrassing imbarazzante [eem-ba-rat-tz*a*n-tay]
embassy l'ambasciata [am-ba-sh*ah*-tah]
emergency emergenza [ay-mayr-j*e*n-tzah]
empty vuoto [vw*o*-toh]
enclose: I enclose . . . accludo . . .
end la fine [f*ee*-nay]
when does it end? quando finisce . . .? [. . . fee-n*ee*-shay]
engaged *(telephone, toilet)* occupato *(person)* fidanzato [fee-dan-tz*ah*-toh]
engagement ring anello di fidanzamento [. . . dee fee-dan-tza-m*e*n-toh]
engine il motore [mo-t*oh*-ray]
engine trouble un guasto al motore [gw*a*s-toh . . .]
England l'Inghilterra [een-gheel-t*e*r-rah]
English inglese [een-gl*ay*-say]
the English gli Inglesi [lee . . .]
do you speak English? parla l'inglese?
enjoy: I enjoyed it very much mi è piaciuto molto [mee eh pee-a-ch*oo*-toh m*o*l-toh]
enlargement *(photo)* un ingrandimento
enormous enorme [ay-n*o*r-may]
enough: thank you, that's enough basta, grazie [. . . gr*ah*-tzee-ay]

entertainment il divertimento [dee-vayr-tee–]
entrance l'entrata
entrata *entrance*
entry l'entrata
envelope una busta [b*oo*s-tah]
equipment l'equipaggiamento [ay-kwee-pa-ja-m*e*n-toh]
error un errore [ayr-r*oh*-ray]
escalator la scala mobile [. . . m*o*-bee-lay]
especially specialmente [spay-chal-m*e*n-tay]
essential essenziale [es-sen-tzee-*ah*-lay]
  it is essential that . . . è indispensabile che . . . [eh een-dees-pen-s*ah*-bee-lay kay]
evacuate evacuare [–ray]
even: even the British perfino gli Inglesi [per-f*ee*-noh lee een-gl*ay*-see]
evening la sera [s*ay*-rah]
  this evening stasera
  in the evening la sera
  good evening buona sera [bw*o*-nah . . .]
  evening dress l'abito da sera [*ah*-bee-toh . . .]
ever: have you ever been to . . .? è mai stato a . . .? [eh m*ah*-ee . . .]
every ogni [*o*n-yee]
  every day ogni giorno [. . . j*o*r-noh]
everyone tutti [t*oo*t-tee]
  everything tutto
  everywhere dappertutto
exact esatto
example esempio [ay-s*e*m-pee-oh]
  for example per esempio
excellent eccellente [ay-chayl-l*e*n-tay]
except: except me eccetto me [ay-ch*e*t-toh may]
excess eccesso [ay-ch*e*s-soh]
  excess baggage bagaglio eccedente [ba-g*a*l-yoh ay-chay-d*e*n-tay]
exchange *(money)* cambio [k*a*m-bee-oh]
  (telephone) il centralino [chen-tra-l*ee*-noh]

exciting entusiasmante [–tay]
how exciting! che bello! [kay . . .]
excursion una gita [*jee*-tah]
excuse me *(to get past)* permesso
(to get attention) scusi [*skoo*-zee]
(apology) mi scusi [mee . . .]
exhaust *(car)* lo scappamento
exhausted sfinito [sfee-*nee*-toh]
exhibition un'esposizione
[ays-po-see-tzee-*oh*-nay]
exhibitor un espositore [–ray]
exit l'uscita [oo-*shee*-tah]
expect: she's expecting è incinta [eh een-*cheen*-tah]
expenses: it's on expenses è a spese della ditta [eh ah *spay*-say *del*-lah *deet*-tah]
expensive costoso
expert esperto
explain spiegare [spee-ay-*gah*-ray]
would you explain that slowly? può spiegarlo lentamente? [pwoh spee-ay-*gar*-loh len-ta-*men*-tay]
export *(noun)* l'esportazione
[ays-por-ta-tzee-*oh*-nay]
exposure meter l'esposimetro
[ays-po-*see*-may-troh]
express espresso
extra *(adjective)*: **an extra day** un altro giorno
is that extra? è extra? [eh . . .]
extremely estremamente [–tay]
eye l'occhio [*ok*-yoh]
eyebrow il sopracciglio [so-pra-*cheel*-yoh]
eyeshadow l'ombretto
eye witness un testimone oculare
[tes-tee-*moh*-nay o-koo-*lah*-ray]
F *(on tap) cold*
face la faccia [*fah*-chah]
face mask *(diving)* la maschera
[*mas*-kay-rah]

fact il fatto
factory la fabbrica [*fa*b-bree-kah]
Fahrenheit il Fahrenheit

» *TRAVEL TIP: to convert F to C:* $F - 32 \times \frac{5}{9} = C$

Fahrenheit	*23*	*32*	*50*	*59*	*70*	*86*	*98.4*
centigrade	*−5*	*0*	*10*	*15*	*21*	*30*	*36.9*

faint: she's fainted è svenuta [eh . . .]
fair una fiera [fee-*ay*-rah]
that's not fair non è giusto [. . . eh j*oo*s-toh]
faithfully: yours faithfully distinti saluti
fake falso
fall: he's fallen è caduto [eh . . .]
false falso
false teeth i denti finti [d*e*n-tee f*ee*n-tee]
family la famiglia [fa-m*ee*l-yah]
fan il ventilatore [ven-tee-la-t*oh*-ray]
(hand-held) un ventaglio [ven-t*a*l-yoh]
(football etc) un tifoso [tee–]
fan-belt la cinghia [ch*ee*n-ghee-ah]
far lontano
is it far? è lontano? [eh . . .]
how far is it? quanto dista? [. . . dees-t*ah*]
fare *(travel)* (il prezzo del) biglietto [pr*e*t-tzoh dayl beel-y*e*t-toh]
farm la fattoria [fat-toh-r*ee*-ah]
farther più lontano [pew . . .]
fashion la moda
fast veloce [vay-l*oh*-chay]
don't speak so fast non parli così in fretta [. . . ko-s*ee* . . .]
fat grasso
fatally fatalmente [–tay]
father: my father mio padre [m*ee*-oh p*ah*-dray]
fathom un braccio [br*ah*-choh]
fault un difetto
it's not my fault non è colpa mia [. . . m*ee*-ah]
faulty difettoso
favourite favorito [fa-vo-r*ee*-toh]

February febbraio [feb-b*rah*-yoh]
fed-up: I'm fed-up sono stufo [. . . st*oo*-foh]
feel: I feel cold/hot ho freddo/caldo [o . . .]
I feel sad sono triste [. . . tr*ee*s-tay]
I feel like . . . ho voglia di . . . [o v*o*l-yah dee]
ferry il traghetto [tra-g*ay*t-toh]
fetch: will you come and fetch me? mi viene a prendere? [mee vee-*ay*-nay ah pr*e*n-day-ray]
fever la febbre [f*e*b-bray]
few: only a few solo pochi [p*o*-kee]
a few days pochi giorni [p*o*-kee j*o*r-nee]
fiancé(e) fidanzato (fidanzata) [fee-dan-tz*ah*-toh . . .]
fiddle: it's a fiddle è un imbroglio [eh oon eem-br*o*l-yoh]
field un campo
figs i fichi [ee f*ee*-kee]
figure *(number)* una cifra [ch*ee*-frah]
I'm watching my figure sto attenta alla linea [. . . l*ee*-nay-ah]
fill: fill her up mi faccia il pieno [mee f*ah*-chah eel pee-*eh*-noh]
to fill in a form riempire un modulo [ree-aym-p*ee*-ray oon m*o*-doo-loh]
fillet il filetto
film *(movie)* un film [feelm]
do you have this type of film? avete questo tipo di pellicola? [a-v*ay*-tay kw*e*s-toh t*ee*-poh dee payl-l*ee*-ko-lah]
filter un filtro
filter/non-filter col filtro/senza filtro
find trovare [tro-v*ah*-ray]
if you find it . . . se lo trova . . . [say . . .]
I've found a . . . ho trovato un . . . [o . . .]
fine: fine weather bel tempo
a 50,000 lire fine una multa di cinquanta mila lire [m*oo*l-tah dee cheen-kw*a*n-tah m*ee*-lah l*ee*-ray]
finger un dito [d*ee*-toh]

fingernail l'unghia [*oo*n-ghee-ah]
finish: I haven't finished non ho finito [non o fee-*nee*-toh]
fire: fire! al fuoco! [fw*o*-koh]
can we light a fire here? possiamo accendere un fuoco qui? [. . . a-*che*n-day-ray oon fw*o*-koh kwee]
it's not firing *(car)* non si accende [non see a-*che*n-day]
fire brigade i vigili del fuoco [ee *vee*-jee-lee del fw*o*-koh]
fire extinguisher un estintore [ays-teen-t*oh*-ray]
» TRAVEL TIP: *in the event of a fire phone 113*
first primo [pr*ee*-moh]
I was first c'ero prima io [ch*eh*-roh pr*ee*-mah *ee*-oh]
first aid il pronto soccorso
first aid kit la cassetta di [dee] pronto soccorso
first class di prima classe [dee pr*ee*-mah kl*a*s-say]
first name il nome di battesimo [n*oh*-may dee bat-t*ay*-see-moh]
fish il pesce [p*ay*-shay]
fishing la pesca
fishing rod la canna da pesca
five cinque [ch*ee*n-kway]
fix: can you fix it? *(repair)* può ripararlo? [pwoh ree-pa-r*a*r-loh]
fizzy gassato
flag la bandiera [ban-dee-*ay*-rah]
flash *(photo)* il flash
flat *(apartment)* un appartamento
(adjective) piatto [pee-*a*t-toh]
this drink is flat questa bibita è svanita [. . . b*ee*-bee-tah eh sva-n*ee*-tah]
I've got a flat (tyre) ho una foratura [o *oo*-nah fo-ra-t*oo*-rah]
flavour il sapore [sa-p*oh*-ray]

flea la pulce [p*oo*l-chay]
flies *(trousers)* la cerniera [chayr-nee-*ay*-rah]
flight il volo
flippers le pinne [lay-p*ee*n-nay]
flirt *(verb)* flirtare [fleer-t*ah*-ray]
float *(verb)* galleggiare [gal-lay-j*ah*-ray]
floor il pavimento
on the second floor al secondo piano
flower un fiore [fee-*oh*-ray]
flu l'influenza [een-floo-*e*n-tzah]
fly *(insect)* una mosca
foggy nebbioso
follow seguire [say-gw*ee*-ray]
food il cibo [ch*ee*-boh] *see pages 70–71*
food poisoning avvelenamento da cibo
fool uno sciocco [sh*o*k-koh]
foot il piede [pee-*ay*-day]
» TRAVEL TIP: *1 foot = 30.1 cm = 0.3 metres*
football *(game)* il calcio [k*a*l-choh]
for per [payr]
forbidden vietato [vee-ay-t*ah*-toh]
foreign straniero [stran-y*eh*-roh]
foreign exchange il cambio estero [k*a*m-bee-oh *e*s-tay-roh]
foreigner uno straniero [stran-y*eh*-roh]
forget dimenticare [dee-men-tee-k*ah*-ray]
I forget, I've forgotten non mi ricordo
don't forget non dimenticare
I'll never forget you non ti dimenticherò mai [non tee dee-men-tee-kay-r*o* m*ah*-ee]
fork la forchetta [for-k*ay*t-tah]
form *(document)* un modulo [m*o*-doo-loh]
formal formale [for-m*ah*-lay]
fortnight due settimane [d*oo*-ay sayt-tee-m*ah* nay]
forward *(adverb)* avanti
could you forward my mail? può inoltrare la mia posta? [pwoh ee-nol-tr*ah*-ray la m*ee*-ah-p*o*s-tah]

foundation cream il fondotinta
fracture una frattura [frat-*too*-rah]
fragile fragile [fr*ah*-jee-lay]
France la Francia [fr*a*n-chah]
free libero [l*ee*-bay-roh] *(no charge)* gratis
admission free ingresso libero
freight *(goods)* le merci [m*ay*r-chee]
French francese [fran-ch*ay*-say]
freshen up: I want to freshen up vorrei darmi una rinfrescata [vor-r*ay* d*a*r-mee . . .]
Friday venerdì [vay-nayr-d*ee*]
fridge il frigo [fr*ee*-goh]
friend un amico [a-m*ee*-koh]
friendly cordiale [kor-dee-*ah*-lay]
from da
where is it from? da dove viene? [dah d*oh*-vay vee-*ay*-nay]
front *(noun)* il davanti
in front of you davanti a lei [. . . lay]
at the front davanti
frost il gelo [j*ay*-loh]
frostbite il congelamento [kon-jay-la-m*e*n-toh]
frozen congelato [kon-jay-l*ah*-toh]
fruit la frutta
fruit salad una macedonia [ma-chay-d*o*n-yah]
fry friggere [fr*ee*-jay-ray]
nothing fried niente di fritto [nee-*e*n-tay dee fr*ee*t-toh]
fried egg un uovo fritto [w*o*-voh . . .]
frying pan una padella
fuel il combustibile [kom-boos-t*ee*-bee-lay]
full pieno [pee-*ay*-noh]
fun: it's fun è divertente [eh dee-vayr-t*e*n-tay]
funny *(comical)* buffo [b*oo*f-foh]
(strange) strano [str*ah*-noh]
furniture il mobilio [mo-b*ee*l-yoh]
further *(adverb)* oltre [*o*l-tray]
fuse un fusibile [foo-s*ee*-bee-lay]

future il futuro [foo-*too*-roh]
in future in futuro
gabinetti *toilets*
gale una bufera [boo-*fay*-rah]
galleria *tunnel*
gallon un gallone [–nay]
» *TRAVEL TIP: 1 gallon = 4.55 litres*
gallstone un calcolo [*ka*l-ko-loh]
gamble *(verb)* giocare d'azzardo [jo-*kah*-ray dat-*tzar*-doh]
gammon il prosciutto affumicato [pro-sh*oo*t-toh af-foo-mee-*kah*-toh]
garage il garage [ga-*rah*-jay]
» *TRAVEL TIP: Italian garages tend to close between 1.00 and 3.00 pm*
garden il giardino [jar-*dee*-noh]
garlic l'aglio [*a*l-yoh]
gas il gas *(petrol)* la benzina [ben-*tzee*-nah]
gas cooker una cucina a gas [koo-*chee*-nah . . .]
gas cylinder la bombola del gas [*bo*m-bo-lah . . .]
gasket la guarnizione [gwar-nee-tzee-*oh*-nay]
gay *(homosexual)* omosessuale [o-mo-ses-soo-*ah*-lay]
gear la marcia [*ma*r-chah]
(equipment) l'attrezzatura [at-tray-tza-*too*-rah]
gearbox la scatola del cambio [*skah*-toh-lah del *ka*m-bee-oh]
gear lever la leva del cambio [*lay*-vah . . .]
I can't get it into gear non riesco ad innestare la marcia [non ree-*ay*s-koh ad een-nes-*tah*-ray . . .]
gents *(toilet)* uomini
» *TRAVEL TIP: only written: ask for* la toilette [twa-*le*t]
German tedesco
Germany la Germania [jayr-*ma*n-yah]
gesture un gesto [*je*s-toh]

get: will you get me a . . .? mi può prendere un . . .? [mee pwoh pr*e*n-day-ray oon . . .]
how do I get to . . .? come faccio per andare a . . .? [k*oh*-may f*ah*-choh payr an-d*ah*-ray ah . . .]
when can I get it back? quando me [may] lo ritorna?
where do I get off? dove scendo? [d*oh*-vay sh*e*n-doh]
when do we get back? quando torniamo?
where can I get a bus for . . .? dove posso prendere un autobus per . . .?
have you got . . .? ha . . .? [ah]
gin il gin
gin and tonic un gin and tonic
girl una ragazza [ra-g*a*t-tzah]
my girlfriend la mia ragazza [m*ee*-ah . . .]
give dare [d*ah*-ray]
will you give me . . .? mi dà . . .? [mee . . .]
I gave it to him gliel'ho dato [lee-*ay*-lo . . .]
glad contento
glandular fever la febbre ghiandolare [f*e*b-bray ghee-an-doh-l*ah*-ray]
glass il vetro
a glass un bicchiere [beek-y*eh*-ray]
glasses gli occhiali [ok-y*ah*-lee]
gloves i guanti [ee gw*a*n-tee]
glue la colla
go: can I have a go? posso provare? [. . . pro-v*ah*-ray]
my car won't go la mia macchina non parte [lah m*ee*-ah m*a*k-kee-nah non p*a*r-tay]
when does the bus go? quando parte l'autobus? [kw*a*n-doh p*a*r-tay l*ow*-toh-boos]
where are you going? dove vai? [d*o*h-vay vah-ee]
the bus has gone l'autobus è partito
he's gone è andato via [eh . . . v*ee*-ah]
goal *(football)* un goal

goat la capra
god il dio [*dee*-oh]
goggles *(skiing)* gli occhiali da neve [lee ok-*yah*-lee da *nay*-vay]
gold l'oro
golf il golf
good buono [*bwo*-noh]
good! bene! [*bay*-nay]
goodbye arrivederci [ar-ree-vay-*dayr*-chee]
gooseberries uva spina [*oo*-vah *spee*-nah]
gramme un grammo
» *TRAVEL TIP: 100 grammes = approx 3½ oz*
grand grandioso [gran-dee-*oh*-soh]
grandfather il nonno
grandmother la nonna
my grandson/granddaughter mio nipote/mia nipote [*mee*-oh nee-*poh*-tay/*mee*-ah . . .]
grapes l'uva [*oo*-vah]
grapefruit il pompelmo
grapefruit juice il succo di pompelmo [*sook*-koh dee]
grass l'erba [*er*-bah]
grateful grato [*grah*-toh]
I'm very grateful to you le sono molto grato [lay . . .]
gravy il sugo [*soo*-goh]
grease il grasso *(car etc)* il lubrificante [loo-bree-fee-*kan*-tay]
greasy unto [*oon*-toh]
great *(big)* grande [. . . day] *(very good)* bellissimo
great! benissimo!
greedy ingordo [een-*gor*-doh]
green verde [*vayr*-day]
greengrocer's il fruttivendolo [froot-tee-*ven*-doh-loh]
green card la carta verde
grey grigio [*gree*-joh]

grilled alla griglia [. . . gr*ee*l-yah]
grocer's una drogheria [dro-gay-r*ee*-ah]
ground: on the ground a terra
on the ground floor a pian terreno [ah pee-*a*n tayr-r*ay*-noh]
group un gruppo [gr*oo*p-poh]
our group leader il nostro capogruppo
I'm with the English group sono con il gruppo degli Inglesi [dayl-yee een-gl*ay*-see]
guarantee: is there a guarantee? ha la garanzia? [ah lah ga-ran-tz*ee*-ah]
guasto *out of order*
guest l'ospite [*o*s-pee-tay]
guesthouse una pensione [payn-see-*oh*-nay]
guide una guida [gw*ee*-dah]
guilty colpevole [kol-p*ay*-vo-lay]
guitar una chitarra [kee-t*a*r-rah]
gums *(in mouth)* le gengive [jen-j*ee*-vay]
gun una pistola [pees-t*oh*-lah]
gynaecologist il ginecologo [jee-nay-k*o*-lo-goh]
hair i capelli *(plural)* [ee . . .]
hairbrush una spazzola per capelli [sp*a*t-tzo-lah . . .]
where can I get a haircut? dove posso farmi tagliare i capelli? [d*oh*-vay pos-soh f*a*r-mee tal-y*ah*-ray . . .]
is there a hairdresser's here? c'è un parrucchiere qui? [cheh oon par-rook-y*ay*-ray kwee]
hairgrip una molletta
half una metà [may-t*ah*]
a half portion una mezza porzione [m*e*t-tzah por-tzee-*oh*-nay]
half an hour mezz'ora
ham il prosciutto [pro-sh*oo*t-toh]
hamburger un hamburger
hammer un martello
hand la mano
handbag la borsetta [bor-s*ay*t-tah]

handbrake il freno a mano
handkerchief il fazzoletto [fat-tzoh-*lay*t-toh]
handle *(door)* la maniglia [ma-*nee*l-yah]
(cup) il manico [m*ah*-nee-koh]
hand luggage il bagaglio a mano
[ba-g*a*l-yoh . . .]
handmade lavorato a mano
handsome bello
hanger la gruccia [gr*oo*-chah]
hangover il mal di [dee] capo (dopo una sbornia)
my head is killing me mi scoppia la testa
happen accadere [ak-ka-d*ay*-ray]
I don't know how it happened non so come è successo [. . . k*oh*-may eh soo-ch*e*s-soh]
what's happening/happened? cosa succede/è successo? [. . . soo-ch*ay*-day . . .]
happy contento
harbour il porto
hard duro [d*oo*-roh]
hard-boiled egg uovo sodo [w*o*-voh . . .]
push hard spinga forte [sp*ee*n-gah f*o*r-tay]
harm il male [m*ah*-lay]
hat il cappello
hate: I hate . . . odio . . . [*o*-dee-oh]
have avere [a-v*ay*-ray]
I have a pain ho un dolore [o oon doh-l*oh*-ray]
do you have any cigars/a map? ha dei sigari/una pianta? [ah day s*ee*-ga-ree . . .]
can I have some water/some more? posso avere dell'acqua/averne ancora? [. . . a-v*ay*r-nay an-k*oh*-rah]
I have to leave tomorrow devo partire domani [d*ay*-voh par-t*ee*-ray doh-m*ah*-nee]
hayfever la febbre da fieno [f*e*b-bray dah fee-*ay*-noh]
he lui [l*oo*-ee]
he is è [eh]
where does he live? dove abita? [d*oh*-vay *ah*-bee-tah]

head la testa
headache il mal di testa [. . . dee . . .]
headlight il faro [*fah*-roh]
head waiter il capocameriere [ka-po-ka-mayr-*yeh*-ray]
head wind un vento di prua [. . . dee pr*oo*-ah]
health la salute [sa-*loo*-tay]
your health! salute!
healthy sano
hear: I can't hear non sento
hearing aid un apparecchio acustico [ap-pa-*ray*k-yoh a-*koo*s-tee-koh]
heart il cuore [kw*o*-ray]
heart attack un colpo al cuore
heat il calore [ka-l*oh*-ray]
heat stroke un colpo di calore [. . . dee . . .]
heating il riscaldamento
heavy pesante [pay-*sa*n-tay]
heel il calcagno [kal-*ka*n-yoh]
(on shoe) il tacco
could you put new heels on these? può mettere i tacchi a questi? [pwoh m*e*t-tay-ray ee t*a*k-kee . . .]
hello ciao [chow]
help *(noun)* aiuto [a-y*oo*-toh]
can you help me? mi può aiutare? [mee pwoh a-yoo-t*ah*-ray]
help! aiuto!
her lei [lay]
have you seen her? l'ha vista? [lah . . .]
will you give it to her? vuole darglielo? [vw*oh*-lay d*a*r-lee-ay-loh]
it's her bag/plate è la sua borsa/il suo piatto
it's hers è sua/suo
here qui [kwee]
high alto
hill la collina [kol-l*ee*-nah]
up/down the hill in salita/discesa [een sa-l*ee*-tah/dee-sh*ay*-sah]

him lui [*loo*-ee]
I know him lo conosco
will you give it to him? vuole darglielo? [vw*oh*-lay d*a*r-lee-ay-loh]
hire *see* **rent**
his il suo [*soo*-oh]; la sua
(plural) i suoi [ee sw*oy*-ee]; le sue [–ay]
it's his è il suo/la sua [eh . . .]
hit: he hit me mi ha colpito [mee ah kol-*pee*-toh]
hitch-hike *(verb)* fare l'autostop [f*ah*-ray l*o*w-toh-st*o*p]
hitch-hiker un autostoppista [ow-toh-stop-*pee*s-tah]
hold tenere [tay-n*ay*-ray]
hole un buco [*boo*-koh]
holiday una vacanza [va-k*a*n-tzah]
I'm on holiday sono in vacanza
home la casa [k*ah*-sah]
I want to go home voglio andare a casa [v*o*l-yoh an-d*ah*-ray . . .]
at home a casa
I am homesick ho nostalgia di casa [o nos-tal-*jee*-ah dee . . .]
honest onesto
honestly? davvero?
honey il miele [mee-*ay*-lay]
honeymoon la luna di miele [. . . dee . . .]
hope *(noun)* la speranza [spay-r*a*n-tzah]
I hope that . . . spero che . . . [sp*ay*-roh kay]
I hope so/not spero di sì/di no [. . . dee see/dee . . .]
horizon l'orizzonte [o-reet-tz*o*n-tay]
horn *(car)* il clacson
horrible orribile [or-*ree*-bee-lay]
hors d'oeuvre l'antipasto
horse il cavallo
hospital l'ospedale [os-pay-d*ah*-lay]
host(ess) l'ospite [*o*s-pee-tay]
air hostess hostess

hot caldo
  (spiced) piccante [peek-k*a*n-tay]
  it's too hot! scotta!
hotel l'albergo
» *TRAVEL TIP: hotels are divided into five categories: de luxe, first, second, third and fourth; hotel lists are issued by the provincial Tourist Board and by the local tourist offices (aziende autonome di soggiorno)*
hotplate il fornello
hot-water bottle la borsa dell'acqua calda
hour l'ora
house la casa [k*ah*-sah]
  housewife la casalinga
how come [k*oh*-may]
  how many? quanti [kw*a*n-tee]
  how much? quanto? [kw*a*n-toh]
  how often do the buses go? con che frequenza partono gli autobus? [kon kay fray-kw*e*n-tzah p*a*r-toh-noh lee *ow*-toh-boos]
  how long does it take? quanto ci impiega? [. . . chee eem-pee-*ay*-gah]
  how long have you been here? da quanto tempo è qua? [. . . eh . . .]
  how are you? come sta? [k*oh*-may stah]
hull lo scafo
humid umido [*oo*-mee-doh]
humour l'umorismo [oo-mo-r*ee*s-moh]
  haven't you got a sense of humour? non ha [ah] il senso dell'umorismo?
hundred cento [ch*e*n-toh]
hundredweight:
» *TRAVEL TIP: 1 cwt = 50.8 kilos*
hungry: I'm hungry/not hungry ho fame/non ho fame [o f*ah*-may . . .]
hurry: I'm in a hurry ho fretta [o fr*a*yt-tah]
  please hurry! per favore faccia presto! [. . . fa-v*oh*-ray f*ah*-chah pr*e*s-toh]
hurt: it hurts fa male [fah m*ah*-lay]

my leg hurts mi fa mal la gamba [mee . . .]
YOU MAY THEN HEAR . . .
è un dolore acuto? [eh oon doh-l*oh*-ray a-k*oo*-toh] *is it a sharp pain?*
husband: my husband mio marito [m*ee*-oh ma-r*ee*-toh]
I io [*ee*-oh]
I am sono
I leave tomorrow parto domani
ice il ghiaccio [ghee-*ah*-choh]
ice-cream il gelato [jay-l*ah*-toh]
iced coffee un caffè freddo [kaf-f*eh* . . .]
with lots of ice con molto ghiaccio
identity papers documenti di identità [. . . dee ee-den-tee-t*ah*]
idiot idiota [ee-dee-*oh*-tah]
if se [say]
ignition l'accensione [a-chayn-see-*oh*-nay]
ill malato
I feel ill mi sento male [mee s*e*n-toh m*ah*-lay]
illegal illegale [eel-lay-g*ah*-lay]
illegible illeggibile [eel-lay-j*ee*-bee-lay]
illness una malattia [ma-lat-t*ee*-ah]
immediately immediatamente [–tay]
import importazione [–*oh*-nay]
important importante [–tay]
it's very important è molto importante
import duty dazio di importazione [d*ah*-tzee-oh dee eem-por-ta-tzee-*oh*-nay]
impossible impossibile [eem-pos-s*ee*-bee-lay]
impressive imponente [–nayn-tay]
improve migliorare [meel-yo-r*ah*-ray]
I want to improve my . . . voglio migliorare il mio . . . [v*o*l-yoh . . . m*ee*-oh]
in in [een]
he'll be here in a while sarà qua fra un po'
in London a Londra
in 1982 nel 1982 [nel m*ee*l-lay-no-vay-ch*e*n-toh-ot-tan-ta-d*oo*-ay]

inch un pollice [pol-lee-chay]
» *TRAVEL TIP: 1 inch = 2.54 cm*
include includere [een-k*loo*-day-ray]
does that include breakfast? è compresa la prima colazione? [eh kom-p*ray*-sah lah p*ree*-mah ko-la-tzee-*oh*-nay]
incompetent incompetente [–tay]
inconsiderate sconsiderato
incontinent incontinente [–tay]
incredible incredibile [–d*ee*-bee-lay]
incrocio *crossroads*
indecent indecente [een-day-ch*e*n-tay]
independent indipendente [–tay]
India l'India [*ee*n-dee-ah]
Indian indiano
indicator la freccia [fr*ay*-chah]
indigestion l'indigestione [–*oh*-nay]
indoors al coperto
industry industria [een-d*oo*s-tree-ah]
infection l'infezione [een-fay-tzee-*oh*-nay]
infectious contagioso [kon-ta-j*oh*-soh]
inflation l'inflazione [een-fla-tzee-*oh*-nay]
informal senza formalità [s*e*n-tzah for-ma-lee-t*ah*]
information: do you have any information in English about . . .? ha delle informazioni in inglese su . . .? [ah d*e*l-lay een-for -ma-tzee-*oh*-nee een een-gl*ay*-say soo]
is there an information office? c'è un ufficio di informazioni? [chay oon oof-f*ee*-choh dee . . .]
ingresso *entrance*
ingresso gratuito, ingresso libero *admission free*
inhabitant un abitante [–tay]
injection l'iniezione [een-yay-tzee-*oh*-nay]
injured ferito [fay-r*ee*-toh]
he's been injured è stato ferito [eh st*ah*-toh . . .]
injury una lesione [lay-see-*oh*-nay]

innocent innocente [een-no-*che*n-tay]
insect un insetto
inside dentro
insist: I insist (on it) insisto [een-*see*s-toh]
insomnia l'insonnia
instant coffee il caffè istantaneo [kaf-*feh* ees-tan-*tah*-nay-oh]
instead invece [een-*vay*-chay]
  instead of . . . invece di [. . . dee]
insulating tape il nastro isolante [. . . ee-so-*la*n-tay]
insulation l'isolamento [ee-so-la-*me*n-toh]
insult un insulto [een-*soo*l-toh]
insurance l'assicurazione [as-see-koo-ra-tzee-*oh*-nay]
intelligent intelligente [–tay]
interesting interessante [–tay]
international internazionale [een-tayr-na-tzee-oh-*nah*-lay]
interpret interpretare [–*tah*-ray]
  would you interpret for us? può farci da interprete? [pwoh *fa*r-chee dah een-*te*r-pray-tay]
into in [een]
introduce: can I introduce . . .? posso presentare . . .? [. . . pray-sayn-*tah*-ray]
invalid *(noun)* un invalido [een-*vah*-lee-doh]
  invalid chair una poltrona da invalido
invitation l'invito [een-*vee*-toh]
  thank you for the invitation grazie dell'invito [*grah*-tzee-ay . . .]
» *TRAVEL TIP: when invited to an Italian house for a meal it is customary to bring a cake or some ice cream, rather than wine*
invite: can I invite you out? vuoi uscire con me? [vwoy oo-*shee*-ray kon may]
invoice la fattura
Ireland l'Irlanda
Irish irlandese [eer-lan-*day*-say]

iron *(clothes)* un ferro da stiro [. . . st*ee*-roh]
will you iron these for me? mi può stirare questi? [mee pwoh stee-*rah*-ray kw*e*s-tee]
ironmonger's una ferramenta
is è [eh]
island l'isola [*ee*-so-lah]
it esso
it's not working non funziona [non foon-tzee-*oh*-nah]
is it . . .? è . . .? [eh]
I'll take it lo prendo
Italian italiano
an Italian woman un'italiana
the Italians gli Italiani [lee . . .]
I don't speak Italian non parlo l'italiano
Italy l'Italia [ee-t*a*l-yah]
itch il prurito [proo-r*ee*-toh]
it itches mi fa prurito [mee . . .]
itemize: would you itemize it for me? me lo dettaglia? [may lo dayt-t*a*l-yah]
IVA *VAT*
jack il cricco [kr*ee*k-koh]
jacket una giacca [j*a*k-kah]
jam la marmellata
traffic jam un ingorgo
January gennaio [jen-n*ah*-yoh]
jaw la mascella [ma-sh*e*l-lah]
jealous geloso [jay-l*oh*-soh]
jeans i jeans
jellyfish una medusa
jetty il molo
jewellery i gioielli [jo-y*e*l-lee]
job un lavoro
that's just the job va proprio a pennello
joke *(noun)* uno scherzo [sk*ay*r-tzoh]
you must be joking sta scherzando
journey un viaggio [vee-*ah*-joh]
have a good journey! buon viaggio! [bwon . . .]

July luglio [*loo*l-yoh]
jumper un maglione [mal-*yoh*-nay]
junction un raccordo
June giugno [*joo*n-yoh]
junk la robaccia [ro-*bah*-chah]
just: just two solo due [*doo*-ay]
just a little solo un po'
it's just there è lì [lee]
not just now per ora no
he was here just now era qua proprio ora
that's just right è proprio giusto [eh *pro*-pree-oh *joo*s-toh]
keen entusiasta [en-too-see-*a*s-tah]
I'm not keen non ne sono entusiasta [. . . nay . . .]
keep: can I keep it? lo posso tenere? [. . . tay-*nay*-ray]
keep the change tenga il resto
you didn't keep your promise non ha mantenuto la promessa [. . . ah . . .]
it keeps on breaking si continua a rompere [see kon-*tee*-noo-ah ah *ro*m-pay-ray]
kettle il bollitore [bol-lee-*toh*-ray]
» *TRAVEL TIP: electric kettles are not generally used in Italy*
key la chiave [kee-*ah*-vay]
kidney il rene [*ray*-nay]
(meat) il rognone [ron-*yoh*-nay]
kill uccidere [oo-*chee*-day-ray]
kilo un chilo [*kee*-loh]
» *TRAVEL TIP: conversion:* $\frac{kilos}{5} \times 11 = pounds$

kilos	*1*	*1½*	*5*	*6*	*7*	*8*	*9*
pounds	*2.2*	*3.3*	*11*	*13.2*	*15.4*	*17.6*	*19.8*

kilometre un chilometro [kee-*loh*-may-troh]
» *TRAVEL TIP: conversion:* $\frac{kilometres}{8} \times 5 = miles$

kilometres	*1*	*5*	*10*	*20*	*50*	*100*
miles	*0.62*	*3.11*	*6.2*	*12.4*	*31*	*62*

kind: that's very kind of you è molto gentile da parte sua [eh . . . jen-*tee*-lay dah *par*-tay . . .]
kiss un bacio [*bah*-choh]
kitchen la cucina [koo-*chee*-nah]
knee il ginocchio [jee-*nok*-yoh]
knickers le mutande [moo-*tan*-day]
knife il coltello [kol-*tel*-loh]
knock bussare [boos-*sah*-ray]
there's a knocking noise from the engine il motore dà dei colpi [eel mo-*toh*-ray dah day *kol*-pee]
know sapere [sa-*pay*-ray]
(be acquainted with) conoscere [ko-*noh*-shay-ray]
I don't know non so
I don't know the area non conosco queste parti [. . . *kwes*-tay *par*-tee]
label l'etichetta [ay-tee-*kayt*-tah]
laces *(shoes)* i lacci [*lah*-chee]
lacquer la lacca
ladies *(toilet)* donne
» *TRAVEL TIP: only written: ask for* la toilette [twa*let*]
lady una signora [seen-*yo*-rah]
lager una birra [*beer*-rah]
lager and lime una birra col succo di cedro [. . . *sook*-koh dee *chay*-droh]
» *TRAVEL TIP: this is an unusual drink in Italy*
lake il lago [*lah*-goh]
lamb l'agnello [an-*yel*-loh]
lamp la lampada [*lam*-pa-dah]
lampshade il paralume [–*loo*-may]
lamp-post il lampione [lam-pee-*oh*-nay]
land *(noun)* la terra
lane *(car)* la corsia [kor-*see*-ah]
language la lingua [*leen*-gwah]
large grande [*gran*-day]
laryngitis la laringite [la-reen-*jee*-tay]
last ultimo [*ool*-tee-moh]

last year/week l'anno scorso/la settimana scorsa
last night la notte scorsa [–tay]
at last! finalmente! [fee-nal-*me*n-tay]
late: sorry I'm late scusi per il ritardo [sk*oo*-zee . . .]
it's a bit late è un po' tardi [eh . . . t*a*r-dee]
please hurry, I'm late in fretta per favore, sono in ritardo [. . . payr fa-v*oh*-ray]
at the latest al più tardi [al pew . . .]
later più tardi
see you later a più tardi
latitude la latitudine [–t*oo*-dee-nay]
laugh *(verb)* ridere [r*ee*-day-ray]
laundrette una lavanderia automatica [la-van-day-r*ee*-ah ow-toh-m*ah*-tee-kah]
» *TRAVEL TIP: if you can't find a laundrette look for a 'lavasecco' (dry-cleaner's)*
lavatory il gabinetto
lavori in corso *men at work*
law la legge [l*eh*-jay]
lawyer l'avvocato
laxative un lassativo
lay-by l'area di parcheggio [*ah*-ray-ah dee par-k*ay*-joh]
lazy pigro [p*ee*-groh]
leaf la foglia [f*o*l-yah]
leak: there's a leak in my ceiling il mio soffitto fa acqua [m*ee*-oh sof-f*ee*t-toh . . .]
it leaks ha una perdita [ah *oo*-nah p*e*r-dee-tah]
learn: I want to learn . . . voglio imparare . . . [v*o*l-yoh eem-pa-r*ah*-ray]
lease *(verb)* affittare [–t*ah*-ray]
least: not in the least proprio per niente [. . . nee-*e*n-tay]
at least almeno [al-m*ay*-noh]
leather la pelle [p*e*l-lay]
leather soles suole di cuoio [sw*o*-lay dee kw*o*-yoh]

leave: we're leaving tomorrow partiamo domani
when does the bus leave? quando parte l'autobus? [. . . *par*-tay *low*-toh-boos]
I left two shirts in my room ho lasciato due camice in camera mia [o la-sh*ah*-toh d*oo*-ay ka-m*ee*-chay een k*ah*-may-rah m*ee*-ah]
can I leave this here? posso lasciarlo qua?
left sinistra [see-n*ee*s-trah]
on the left a sinistra
left-handed mancino [man-ch*ee*-noh]
left luggage (office) il deposito bagagli [day-p*o*-see-toh ba-g*a*l-yee]
leg la gamba
legal legale [lay-g*ah*-lay]
lemon un limone [lee-m*oh*-nay]
lemonade una limonata [lee-mo-n*ah*-tah]
lend: will you lend me your . . .? mi presta il suo . . .? [mee . . .]
lengthen allungare [al-loon-g*ah*-ray]
lens la lente [l*e*n-tay]
Lent la Quaresima [kwa-r*ay*-see-mah]
less meno [m*ay*-noh]
less than meno di [. . . dee]
less than you think meno che non pensi [. . . kay . . .]
let: let me help aspetti che l'aiuto [. . . kay la-y*oo*-toh]
let me go! mi lasci andare! [mee l*ah*-shee an-d*ah*-ray]
will you let me off here? mi fa scendere qua? [mee fah sh*e*n-day-ray . . .]
let's go andiamo
let me have a look mi faccia vedere [mee f*ah*-chah vay-d*ay*-ray]
letter la lettera [l*e*t-tay-rah]
are there any letters for me? ci sono lettere per me? [chee . . . may]
letterbox la cassetta delle lettere [. . . –ray]

lettuce l'insalata
level-crossing passaggio a livello [pas-*sah*-joh ah lee-*vel*-loh]
liable *(responsible)* responsabile [res-pon-*sah*-bee-lay]
libero *vacant*
library la biblioteca [bee-blee-o-*tay*-kah]
licence il permesso
lid il coperchio [ko-*per*-kee-oh]
lie *(noun)* la menzogna [mayn-*tzon*-yah]
  can he lie down for a bit? può andare a riposarsi per un po'? [pwoh an-*dah*-ray . . .]
life la vita [*vee*-tah]
  life assurance l'assicurazione sulla vita [as-see-koo-ra-tzee-*oh*-nay *sool*-lah . . .]
  lifebelt/life-jacket la cintura di salvataggio [cheen-*too*-rah dee sal-va-*tah*-joh]
  lifeboat la scialuppa di salvataggio [sha-*loop*-pah dee . . .]
  life-guard il bagnino [ban-*yee*-noh]
lift: do you want a lift? vuole un passaggio? [*vwoh*-lay oon pas-*sah*-joh]
  could you give me a lift? mi può dare un passaggio? [mee pwoh *dah*-ray . . .]
  the lift isn't working l'ascensore non funziona [la-shayn-*soh*-ray non foon-tzee-*oh*-nah]
light *(not heavy)* leggero [lay-*jay*-roh]
  the lights aren't working la luce non funziona [la *loo*-chay non foon-tzee-*oh*-nah]
  (car) i fari non funzionano [ee *fah*-ree non foon-tzee-*oh*-na-noh]
  have you got a light? ha da accendere? [ah da a-*chen*-day-ray]
  when it gets light quando fa giorno [. . . *jor*-noh]
  light bulb la lampadina [–*dee*-nah]
  light meter l'esposimetro [les-po-*see*-may-troh]

like: would you like . . .? vuole . . .? [vw*oh*-lay]
I'd like a coffee vorrei un caffè [vor-r*ay* oon kaf-f*eh*]
I'd like to go vorrei partire [. . . –t*ee*-ray]
I like you mi sei simpatico [mee say seem-p*ah*-tee-koh]
I like it/I don't like it mi piace/non mi piace [. . . mee pee-*ah*-chay]
what's it like? com'è? [koh-m*eh*]
one like this uno come questo [. . . k*o*h-may . . .]
do it like this lo faccia così [lo f*ah*-chah ko-s*ee*]
lime il cedro [ch*ay*-droh]
line la linea [l*ee*-nay-ah]
lips le labbra
lipstick il rossetto
lip salve il burro di cacao [b*oo*r-roh dee ka-k*ah*-oh]
liqueur un liquore [lee-kw*oh*-ray]
» *TRAVEL TIP:* ***Sambuca:*** *sort of anisette;* ***amaro:*** *bitter, made with herbs;* ***Fernet:*** *rather medicinal flavour, great for upset stomach or hangover;* ***Strega:*** *unique flavour, herb-based*
list *(noun)* la lista
listen ascoltare [–t*ah*-ray]
litre un litro
» *TRAVEL TIP: 1 litre = $1\frac{3}{4}$ pints = 0.22 gals*
little *(adjective)* piccolo
a little ice/a little more un po' di ghiaccio/un po' di più [. . . dee ghee-*ah*-choh/. . . dee pew]
just a little solo un po'
live vivere [v*ee*-vay-ray]
I live in Glasgow/in England abito a Glasgow/in Inghilterra [*ah*-bee-toh . . . een-gheel-t*e*r-rah]
where do you live? dove abita? [d*oh*-vay *ah*-bee-tah]
liver il fegato [f*ay*-ga-toh]
lizard la lucertola [loo-ch*ay*r-toh-lah]
loaf una pagnotta [pan-y*o*t-tah]

lobster l'aragosta
local: could we try a local wine? possiamo provare un vino locale? [. . . pro-*vah*-ray oon *vee*-noh lo-*kah*-lay]
a local restaurant un ristorante locale
is it made locally? è fatto sul posto? [eh . . .]
lock la serratura
the lock's broken la serratura è rotta
I've locked myself out mi sono chiuso fuori [mee *soh*-noh kee-*oo*-soh *fwoh*-ree]
London Londra
lonely: are you lonely? ti senti solo? [tee . . .]
long lungo [*loo*n-goh]
we'd like to stay longer vorremmo stare più a lungo [. . . *stah*-ray pew . . .]
that was long ago questo era tanto tempo fa [. . . *eh*-rah]
longitude la longitudine [lon-jee-*too*-dee-nay]
loo: where's the loo? dov'è il gabinetto? [doh-*veh* . . .]
look: you look tired mi sembra stanco [mee . . .]
I'm looking forward to . . . non vedo l'ora di . . . [. . . *vay*-doh . . . dee]
I'm just looking sto guardando [. . . gwar-*da*n-doh]
I'm looking for . . . cerco . . . [*chay*r-koh]
look at that guarda quello [*gwa*r-dah . . .]
look out! attento!
loose allentato
(clothes) largo
lorry l'autocarro [ow-toh-*ka*r-roh]
lorry-driver il camionista
lose perdere [*pay*r day-ray]
I've lost my . . . ho perso il mio . . . [o *pay*r-soh eel *mee*-oh]
excuse me, I'm lost scusi, mi sono perso [*skoo*-zee, mee . . .]

lost property (office) oggetti smarriti [o-*jet*-tee smar-*ree*-tee]
lot: a lot/not a lot molto/non molto
a lot of chips/wine tante patatine/tanto vino [*tan*-tay pa-ta-*tee*-nay/*tan*-toh *vee*-noh]
lots (of) un sacco (di) [. . . dee]
a lot more expensive molto più caro [. . . pew . . .]
lotion la lozione [lo-tzee-*oh*-nay]
loud: could you speak louder? può parlare più forte? [pwoh par-*lah*-ray pew *for*-tay]
love: I love you ti amo [tee *ah*-moh]
do you love me? mi ami? [mee *ah*-mee]
he's in love è innamorato [eh . . .]
I love this wine questo vino mi piace moltissimo [*kwes*-toh *vee*-noh mee pee-*ah*-chay . . .]
lovely bello
low basso
luck fortuna [for-*too*-nah]
good luck! buona fortuna! [*bwo*-nah . . .]
lucky fortunato [for-too-*nah*-toh]
you're lucky sei fortunato [say . . .]
that's lucky che fortuna [kay . . .]
luggage il bagaglio [ba-*gal*-yoh]
lumbago la lombaggine [lom-*bah*-jee-nay]
lump *(in the body)* un gonfiore [gon-fee-*oh*-ray]
lunch il pranzo [*pran*-tzoh]
(in Rome) la colazione [–tzee-*oh*-nay]
lung il polmone [pol-*moh*-nay]
luxurious lussuoso
luxury il lusso [*loos*-soh]
a luxury hotel un albergo di [dee] lusso
mad matto
madam signora [seen-*yoh*-rah]
made-to-measure fatto su misura [. . . soo mee-*soo*-rah]
magazine una rivista [ree-*vees*-tah]
magnificent magnifico [man-*yee*-fee-koh]

maiden name il nome da signorina [n*oh*-may dah seen-yo-r*ee*-nah]
mail la posta; **is there any mail for me?** c'è posta per me? [cheh . . . may]
mainland il continente [–n*e*n-tay]
main road la strada principale [. . . preen-chee-p*ah*-lay]
make fare [f*ah*-ray]
will we make it in time? ce la faremo in tempo? [chay la fa-r*ay*-moh . . .]
make-up il trucco [tr*oo*k-koh]
man un uomo [w*o*-moh]
manager il direttore [dee-ray-t*oh*-ray]
can I see the manager? posso parlare col direttore? [. . . par-l*ah*-ray . . .]
manicure una manicure [ma-nee-k*oo*-ray]
manners le maniere [man-y*ay*-ray]
haven't you got any manners? non ha un po' di educazione? [non ah oon po dee ay-doo-ka-tzee-*oh*-nay]
many molti [m*o*l-tee]
map: a map of Italy una carta d'Italia
a map of Rome una pianta di Roma [pee-*a*n-tah dee . . .]
March marzo [m*a*r-tzoh]
margarine la margarina [mar-ga-r*ee*-nah]
marina il porto turistico [. . . too-r*ee*s-tee-koh]
mark: there's a mark on it c'è un segno [cheh oon s*ay*n-yoh]
market place il mercato [mayr-k*ah*-toh]
marmalade la marmellata d'arance [mar-mel-l*ah*-tah da-r*an*-chay]
married sposato
marry: will you marry me? mi vuoi sposare? [mee vw*oy*-ee spo-s*ah*-ray]
marvellous meraviglioso [may-ra-veel *yoh*-soh]
mascara il mascara
mashed potatoes il purè di patate [poo-r*e*h dee pa-t*ah*-tay]

massage il massaggio [mas-*sah*-joh]
mast l'albero [al-bay-roh]
mat *(door)* lo stuoino [stwo-*ee*-noh]
(table) un sottopiatto
match un fiammifero [fee-am-m*ee*-fay-roh]
(short waxed match used by smokers) un cerino [chay-r*ee*-noh]
a box of matches una scatola di fiammiferi [sk*ah*-toh-lah dee . . .]
football match una partita di calcio [par-t*ee*-tah dee k*a*l-choh]
material la stoffa
matter: it doesn't matter non importa
what's the matter? cosa c'è? [. . . cheh]
mattress il materasso
mature maturo [ma-t*oo*-roh]
maximum massimo [m*a*s-see-moh]
May maggio [m*ah*-joh]
may: may I have . . .? potrei avere . . .? [po-tr*ay* a-v*ay*-ray]
maybe forse [f*o*r-say]
mayonnaise la maionese [mah-yo-n*ay*-say]
me: with me con me [kon may]
he knows me mi conosce [mee ko-n*oh*-shay]
it's me sono io [. . . *ee*-oh]
meal il pasto
mean: what does this mean? cosa vuol dire? [. . . vwol d*ee*-ray]
by all means! certamente! [chayr-ta-m*e*n-tay]
measles il morbillo
German measles la rosolia [ro-so-l*ee*-ah]
measurements le misure [mee-s*oo*-ray]
meat la carne [k*a*r-nay]
mechanic: is there a mechanic here? c'è un meccanico qui? [cheh oon mayk-k*ah*-nee-koh kwee]
medicine la medicina [may-dee-ch*ee*-na]
Mediterranean il Mediterraneo [–r*ah*-nay-oh]
meet: when shall we meet? a che ora ci

ritroviamo? [ah kay *oh*-rah chee . . .]
I met him in the street l'ho incontrato per strada [lo . . .]; **pleased to meet you** piacere [pee-ah-ch*ay*-ray]
meeting un incontro
melon un melone [may-l*oh*-nay]
member un socio [so-choh]
how do I become a member? come si diventa soci? [k*oh*-may see dee-ven-tah so-chee]
men gli uomini [lee wo-mee-nee]
mend: can you mend this? può aggiustare questo? [pwoh a-joos-t*ah*-ray . . .]
mention: don't mention it prego [pr*ay*-goh]
menu il menù [may-n*oo*]
can I have the menu, please? posso avere il menù, per favore? [. . . a-v*ay*-ray . . . payr fa-v*oh*-ray]
» *TRAVEL TIP: see pages 70–71*
mess: what a mess! che pasticcio! [kay pas-t*ee*-choh]
my room is in a mess la mia camera è in disordine [lah m*ee*-ah k*ah*-may-rah eh een dee-s*or*-dee-nay]
message: are there any messages for me? ci sono messaggi per me? [chee s*oh*-noh mays-s*ah*-jee payr may]
can I leave a message for . . .? posso lasciare un messaggio per . . .? [. . . la-sh*ah*-ray . . .]
metre un metro [m*ay*-troh]
» *TRAVEL TIP: 1 metre = 39.37 ins = 1.09 yds*
metropolitana *underground*
midday mezzogiorno [met-tzo-jor-noh]
middle mezzo [met-tzoh]
in the middle nel mezzo
midnight mezzanotte [met-tza-not-tay]
might: I might be late può darsi che faccia tardi [pwoh d*a*r-see kay f*ah*-chah t*a*r-dee]
he might have gone può darsi che se ne sia andato [. . . kay say nay s*ee*-ah an-d*ah*-toh]

Antipasti: Starters
affettati misti *assorted cold meats*
prosciutto e melone *ham and melon*
insalata di frutti di mare *seafood salad*

Primi piatti: Soups and pasta
stracciatella *clear soup with eggs and cheese*
minestrone *thick vegetable soup*
zuppa di pesce *fish soup*
spaghetti alla carbonara *with egg and bacon sauce*
spaghetti al sugo *with meat sauce*
spaghetti al pomodoro *with tomato sauce*
lasagne al forno *layers of pasta and meat sauce covered with cheese and baked*
cannelloni *pasta stuffed with meat sauce and baked*
ravioli *pasta squares stuffed with meat or other savoury filling, served with a sauce*
gnocchi *potato dumplings*
risotto alla milanese *rice cooked in white wine and saffron with mushrooms and cheese*

Carni: Meat dishes
bistecca ai ferri/alla pizzaiola/alla fiorentina *grilled steak/steak with tomato sauce/grilled T-bone steak*
cotoletta alla milanese *veal cutlet in egg and breadcrumbs*
cotoletta d'agnello/di vitello *lamb/veal cutlet*
ossobuco *knuckle of veal in wine and tomato sauce*
saltimbocca alla romana *veal escalopes with ham and sage*
spezzatino di vitello *veal stew*

Pollame: Poultry
anitra all'arancio *duck in orange sauce*
pollo arrosto *roast chicken*
pollo alla cacciatora *chicken in a wine, onion and tomato sauce*

Pesce: Fish
baccalà *salt cod*
calamari in umido *squid in wine, garlic and tomato sauce*
fritto misto *mixed fried fish*
polipo ai ferri *grilled octopus*
sogliola al burro *sole in butter sauce*
trota ai ferri *grilled trout*

Contorni: Vegetables
patate: arrosto/fritte/cotte *potatoes: roast/fried/boiled*
puré di patate *mashed potatoes*
insalata mista *mixed salad*
pomodori al gratin *grilled tomatoes*
fagiolini al burro *French beans in butter*
finocchi al forno *fennel with cheese, browned in the oven*
melanzane al forno *baked aubergines in cheese sauce*
zucchini fritti *fried courgettes*

Formaggi: Cheese
Bel Paese *soft, full fat cheese*
caciotta *hard, medium fat cheese*
gorgonzola *soft, tangy blue cheese*
mozzarella *soft, sweet cheese made from buffalo's milk*
parmigiano *Parmesan*

Frutta e dolci: Desserts
macedonia *fruit salad*
bignè *profiteroles*
cassata *ice cream with candied fruit*
gelato *ice cream*
torta di mele/ciliege etc *apple/cherry etc tart*
zabaione *frothy dessert made with egg yolks, sugar and marsala wine*
zuppa inglese *trifle*

migraine l'emicrania [ay-mee-k*ra*n-yah]
mild *(weather)* mite [m*ee*-tay]
(cheese) dolce [d*o*l-chay]
mile un miglio [m*ee*l-yoh]

» *TRAVEL TIP: conversion:* $\frac{miles}{5} \times 8 = kilometres$

miles	½	*1*	*3*	*5*	*10*	*50*	*100*
kilometres	*0.8*	*1.6*	*4.8*	*8*	*16*	*80*	*160*

milk il latte [l*a*t-tay]
a glass of milk un bicchiere di latte [oon beek-*yeh*-ray dee . . .]
milkshake un frappé [frap-p*ay*]
millimetre un millimetro [meel-l*ee*-may-troh]
million un milione [meel-y*o*-nay]
milometer il contachilometri [–kee-l*o*-may-tree]
minced meat la carne tritata [k*a*r-nay tree-t*ah*-tah]
mind: I've changed my mind ho cambiato idea [o kam-bee-*ah*-toh ee-d*ay*-ah]
I don't mind non importa
I don't mind driving sono disposto a guidare [. . . gwee-d*ah*-ray]
do you mind if I . . .? le spiace se . . .? [lay spee-*ah*-chay say]
never mind non fa niente [. . . nee-*e*n-tay]
mine mio [m*ee*-oh]
that's mine questo è mio
mineral water l'acqua minerale [–r*ah*-lay]
minimum minimo [m*ee*-nee-moh]
minus meno [m*ay*-noh]
it's minus 3 degrees ci sono tre gradi sotto zero [chee s*oh*-noh tray gr*ah*-dee s*o*t-toh tz*ay*-roh]
minute minuto [mee-n*oo*-toh]
in a minute subito [s*oo*-bee-toh]
just a minute un momento
mirror lo specchio [sp*e*k-yoh]
Miss signorina [seen-yoh-r*ee*-nah]

miss: I miss you mi manchi [mee-*ma*n-kee]
Carlo's missing manca Carlo
there's a . . . missing manca un . . .
mist la foschia [fos-*kee*-ah]
mistake uno sbaglio [sb*a*l-yoh]
I think you've made a mistake credo che si sia sbagliato [kr*ay*-doh kay see *see*-ah sbal-*yah*-toh]
misunderstanding un malinteso [–*tay*-soh]
modern moderno [–*ay*r-noh]
Monday lunedì [loo-nay-*dee*]
money il denaro
I've lost my money ho perso i soldi [o p*ay*r-soh ee s*o*l-dee]
I've got no money sono senza soldi [. . . s*e*n-tzah . . .]
month un mese [m*ay*-say]
moon la luna [l*oo*-nah]
moorings gli ormeggi [lee or-m*ay*-jee]
moped il motorino [–*ree*-noh]
more più [pew]
can I have some more? posso averne ancora? [. . . a-v*ay*r-nay . . .]
more wine, please ancora del vino per favore [. . . *vee*-noh payr fa-v*oh*-ray]
no more basta [b*a*s-tah]
more comfortable più comodo
more than più di [. . . dee]
morning il mattino [–*tee*-noh]
good morning buon giorno [bwon j*o*r-noh]
this morning questa mattina
in the morning di mattina [dee . . .]
tomorrow morning domattina
mosquito una zanzara
most: I like it the most mi piace più di tutto [mee pee-*ah*-chay pew dee t*oo*t-toh]
I like you the most mi piaci più di tutti [. . . pee-*ah*-chee . . .]
most of the time la maggior parte del tempo

[ma-*jo*r *pa*r-tay . . .]
most of the people il più della gente [*de*l-lah *je*n-tay]
motel un motel
mother: my mother mia madre [m*ee*-ah m*ah*-dray]
motor il motore [–ray]
motorbike la motocicletta [–chee-kl*ay*t-tah]
motorboat il motoscafo
motorcyclist il motociclista [–chee-kl*ee*s-tah]
motorist un automobilista [ow-toh-mo-bee-l*ee*s-tah]
motorway l'autostrada [ow-toh-str*ah*-dah]
mountain la montagna [mon-t*a*n-yah]
mountaineer un alpinista
mountaineering l'alpinismo
mouse un topo
moustache i baffi [ee . . .]
mouth la bocca
move: don't move non si muova [non see mw*o*-vah]
could you move your car? può spostare la macchina? [pw*o*h spos-t*ah*-ray lah m*a*k-kee-nah]
Mr signor, Sig. [seen-y*o*r]
Mrs signora, Sig.ra [seen-y*o*-rah]
Ms *no equivalent*
much molto
much better/much more molto meglio/molto di più [. . . m*e*l-yoh . . . dee pew]
not much non molto
mug: I've been mugged sono stato assalito e derubato [. . . st*ah*-toh as-sa-l*ee*-toh ay day-roo-b*ah*-toh]
mum mamma
muscle il muscolo [m*oo*s-ko-loh]
museum il museo [moo-s*eh*-oh]
mushrooms i funghi [f*oo*n-ghee]
music la musica [m*oo*-see-kah]

must: I must have . . . devo avere . . . [d*ay*-voh a-v*ay*-ray]
I must not eat . . . non devo mangiare . . . [man-j*ah*-ray]
you must do it deve farlo [d*ay*-vay . . .]
must I . . .? devo . . .?
mustard la senape [s*ay*-na-pay]
my il mio [m*ee*-oh]; la mia; *(plural)* i miei [ee mee-*eh*-ee]; le mie [–ay]
nail *(finger)* l'unghia [*oo*n-ghee-ah]
(wood) il chiodo [kee-*o*-doh]
nail clippers un tagliaunghie [tal-yah-*oo*n-ghee-ay]
nail file la limetta da unghie [lee-m*ay*t-tah . . .]
nail polish lo smalto per unghie
nail scissors le forbicine da unghie [for-bee-ch*ee*-nay]
naked nudo [n*oo*-doh]
name il nome [n*oh*-may]
my name is . . . mi chiamo . . . [mee kee-*ah*-moh]
what's your name? come si chiama? [k*oh*-may see kee-*ah*-mah]
napkin il tovagliolo [toh-val-y*o*-loh]
nappy il pannolino [pan-no-l*ee*-noh]
narrow stretto
national nazionale [na-tzee-oh-n*ah*-lay]
nationality la nazionalità [–tah]
natural naturale [na-too-r*ah*-lay]
naughty: don't be naughty non essere impertinente [non *e*s-say-ray . . . –tay]
near: is it near? è vicino? [eh vee-ch*ee*-noh]
near here qui vicino [kwee . . .]
do you go near . . .? va dalle parti di . . .? [vah d*a*l-lay p*a*r-tee dee]
where's the nearest . . .? dov'è il più vicino . . .? [doh-v*eh* il pew . . .]
nearly quasi [kw*ah*-see]

neat *(drink)* liscio [*lee*-shoh]
necessary necessario [nay-chays-*sah*-ree-oh]
it's not necessary non è necessario
neck il collo
necklace la collana
need: I need a . . . ho bisogno di . . .
[o bee-*so*nn-yoh dee]
needle un ago [*ah*-goh]
negotiations le trattative [lay trat-ta-*tee*-vay]
neighbour il vicino [vee-*chee*-noh]
neither: neither of them nessuno dei due
[. . . day *doo*-ay]
neither . . . nor . . . né . . . né . . . [nay . . . nay . . .]
neither do I neanche io [nay-*a*n-kay *ee*-oh]
nephew: my nephew mio nipote [*mee*-oh nee-*poh*-tay]
nervous nervoso
net la rete [*ray*-tay]
net price prezzo netto [*pre*t-tzoh]
never mai [*mah*-ee]
well, I never! perbacco! [payr–]
I never go there non ci vado mai [. . . chee *vah*-doh . . .]
new nuovo [*nwo*-voh]
New Year l'Anno Nuovo
Happy New Year! Buon Anno! [bwon . . .]
New Year's Eve la sera di Capodanno
[. . . *say*-rah dee . . .]
New Zealand la Nuova Zelanda
[. . . tzay-*lan*-dah]
New Zealander un neozelandese
[nay-oh-tzay-lan-*day*-say]
news le notizie [no-*tee*-tzee-ay]
newsagent il giornalaio [jor-na-*lah*-yoh]
newspaper il giornale [jor-*nah*-lay]
do you have any English newspapers? ha dei giornali inglesi? [ah day jor-*nah*-lee een-*glay*-see]

next: the next day il giorno dopo [*jo*r-noh . . .]
sit next to me si sieda vicino a me [see see-*eh*-dah vee-ch*ee*-noh ah may]
please stop at the next corner per favore si fermi al prossimo angolo [payr fa-v*oh*-ray see f*e*r-mee al pr*o*s-see-moh *a*n-go-loh]
see you next year arrivederci all'anno prossimo [ar-ree-vay-d*ay*r-chee . . .]
nice: a nice person una persona simpatica [. . . seem-p*ah*-tee-kah]
a nice day una bella giornata [. . . jor-n*ah*-tah]
niece: my niece mia nipote [m*ee*-ah nee-p*oh*-tay]
night la notte [n*o*t-tay]
good night buona notte [bw*o*-nah . . .]
at night di notte [dee . . .]
is there a good night club here? c'è un buon night club qua? [cheh oon bwon . . .]
nightdress la camicia da notte [ka-m*ee*-chah . . .]
night porter il portiere di notte [por-tee-*ay*-ray dee . . .]
nine nove [n*o*-vay]
nineteen diciannove [dee-chan-n*o*-vay]
nineteen eighty two/three millenovecentoottantadue/tré [m*ee*l-lay-no-vay-ch*e*n-toh-ot-tan-ta-d*oo*-ay/tr*ay*]
no no
there's no water non c'è acqua [non cheh . . .]
no way! certamente no! [chayr-ta-m*e*n-tay . . .]
I've no money non ho denaro [. . . o . . .]
nobody nessuno
nobody saw it non l'ha visto nessuno [non lah . . .]
noisy rumoroso
our room's too noisy la nostra camera è troppo rumorosa [. . . k*ah*-may-rah eh . . .]

non toccare *do not touch*
none nessuno
none of them nessuno di essi [. . . dee *e*s-see]
nonsense sciocchezze [shok-k*ay*t-tzay]
normal normale [nor-m*ah*-lay]
north nord
Northern Ireland l'Irlanda del Nord
nose il naso
nosebleed il sangue al naso [s*a*n-gway . . .]
not non
I'm not hungry non ho fame [non o f*ah*-may]
not that one non quello
not me io no [*ee*-oh . . .]
I don't smoke non fumo [non f*oo*-moh]
I didn't order it non l'ho ordinato [non lo . . .]
note *(bank note)* una banconota
nothing niente [nee-*e*n-tay]
November novembre [–bray]
now adesso
nowhere da nessuna parte [. . . p*a*r-tay]
nudist il nudista [noo-d*ee*s-tah]
nudist beach la spiaggia per nudisti [spee-*ah*-jah . . .]
nuisance: it's a nuisance! è una seccatura! [eh . . .]
this man's being a nuisance quest'uomo sta dando fastidio [kwest-w*o*-moh . . . fas-t*ee*-dee-oh]
numb intorpidito [een-tor-pee-d*ee*-toh]
number il numero [n*oo*-may-roh] *see page 128*
number plate la targa
nurse l'infermiera [een-fer-mee-*ay*-rah]
nursery slope *(skiing)* la pista per principianti [p*ee*s-tah payr preen-cheep-y*a*n-tee]
nut la noce [n*oh*-chay]
(for bolt) il dado [d*ah*-doh]
oar il remo [r*ay*-moh]
obligatory obbligatorio [–t*oh*-ree-oh]
obviously ovviamente [–m*e*n-tay]

occasionally a volte [vol-tay]
occupato *engaged*
occupied: is this seat occupied? è occupato? [eh . . .]
o'clock *see* **time**
October ottobre [ot-*toh*-bray]
octopus il polipo [po-lee-poh]
odd *(number)* dispari [*dees*-pa-ree]
(strange) strano
of di [dee]
off: the milk/meat is off il latte è andato/la carne è andata a male [eel *lat*-tay eh an-*dah*-toh/la *kar*-nay eh an-*dah*-tah ah *mah*-lay]
it just came off si è staccato [see . . .]
10% off uno sconto del dieci per cento [. . . dee-*ay*-chee payr *chen*-toh]
offence un'offesa
office l'ufficio [oof-*fee*-choh]
official *(noun)* un ufficiale [oof-fee-*chah*-lay]
often spesso
oil l'olio [*ol*-yoh]
I'm losing oil perdo l'olio
will you change the oil? mi cambia l'olio? [mee *kam*-bee-ah . . .]
ointment la pomata
OK okay
old vecchio [*vek*-yoh]
how old are you? quanti anni hai? [*kwan*-tee *an*-nee *ah*-ee]
olive l'oliva [o-*lee*-vah]
olive oil l'olio d'oliva [*ol*-yoh . . .]
omelette la frittata
on su [soo]
I haven't got it on me non l'ho qui [non lo kwee]
on Friday venerdì [–dee]
on television alla televisione [. . . tay-lay-vee-see-*oh*-nay]

once una volta
at once subito [*soo*-bee-toh]
one uno
the red one quello rosso
onion una cipolla [chee-*pol*-lah]
only solo
the only one l'unico [*loo*-nee-koh]
open *(adjective)* aperto
I can't open it non riesco ad aprirlo [non ree-*ays*-koh . . .]
when do you open? a che ora aprite? [ah kay *oh*-rah a-*pree*-tay]
opera l'opera [*o*-pay-rah]
operation l'operazione [o-pay-ra-tzee-*oh*-nay]
will I need an operation? ho bisogno di una operazione? [o bee-*sonn*-yoh dee . . .]
operator *(phone)* il centralino [chen-tra-*lee*-noh]
» *TRAVEL TIP: for information dial 181*
opposite: opposite the hotel davanti all'albergo
optician l'ottico
or o
orange *(fruit)* l'arancia [a-*ran*-chah]
(colour) arancione [a-ran-ch*oh*-nay]
orange juice succo d'arancia [*soo*k-koh . . .]
order: could we order now? possiamo ordinare adesso? [. . . or-dee-*nah*-ray . . .]
thank you, we've already ordered grazie, abbiamo già ordinato [*grah*-tzee-ay ab-bee-*ah*-moh djah . . .]
other: the other one quell'altro
do you have any others? ne ha degli altri? [nay ah d*ay*-lee *al*-tree]
otherwise altrimenti [–tee]
ought: I ought to go dovrei andare [doh-vr*ay* an-d*ah*-ray]
ounce un'oncia [*on*-chah]
» *TRAVEL TIP: 1 ounce = 28.35 grammes*

our il nostro; la nostra
that's ours è nostro
out: we're out of petrol siamo senza benzina [see-*ah*-moh *sen*-tzah ben-*tzee*-nah]
get out! fuori! [fw*oh*-ree]
outboard *(motor)* il fuoribordo [fwo-ree-*bor*-doh]
outdoors all'aperto
outside: can we sit outside? possiamo sederci fuori? [. . . say-*dayr*-chee fw*oh*-ree]
over: over here/there qui/la [kwee/lah]
he's over 40 ha più di quarant'anni [ah pew dee kwa-ran-*tan*-nee]
it's all over è tutto finito [eh . . .]
overboard: man overboard! uomo in mare! [*wo*-moh een *mah*-ray]
overcharge: you've overcharged me mi ha fatto pagare troppo [mee ah *fat*-toh pa-*gah*-ray . . .]
overcooked troppo cotto
overexposed sovraesposto [so-vra-ays-*pos*-toh]
overnight *(stay)* per una notte [. . . *not*-tay]
we've travelled overnight abbiamo viaggiato di notte [. . . vee-a-*jah*-toh dee . . .]
oversleep: I overslept non mi sono svegliato [non mee *soh*-noh svayl-*yah*-toh]
overtake sorpassare [sor-pas-*sah*-ray]
owe: what do I owe you? quanto le devo? [. . . lay *day*-voh]
own *(adjective)* proprio [*pro*-pree-oh]
my own . . . il mio proprio . . . [*mee*-oh . . .]
I'm on my own sono da solo
owner il proprietario [pro-pree-ay-*tah*-ree-oh]
oxygen l'ossigeno [os-*see*-jay-noh]
oysters le ostriche [*os*-tree-kay]
pack: I haven't packed yet non ho ancora fatto i bagagli [ee ba-*gal*-yee]
can we have a packed lunch? potremmo avere un cestino da viaggio? [. . . a-*vay*-ray oon

ches-*tee*-noh dah vee-*ah*-joh]
package tour il viaggio organizzato [vee-*ah*-joh or-ga-neet-*tzah*-toh]
page *(of book)* la pagina [*pah*-jee-nah]
could you page him? può farlo cercare? [pwoh *far*-loh chayr-*kah*-ray]
pain il dolore [doh-*loh*-ray]
I've got a pain in my . . . ho [o] un dolore al . . .
painkillers gli analgesici [lee a-nal-*jay*-see-chee]
painting un dipinto [dee-*peen*-toh]
pair un paio [*pah*-yoh]
Pakistan il Pakistan
Pakistani pakistano
pale pallido [*pal*-lee-doh]
pancake la frittella
panties le mutandine [moo-tan-*dee*-nay]
pants i pantaloni [ee . . .]
(underpants) le mutande [moo-*tan*-day]
paper la carta
(newspaper) il giornale [jor-*nah*-lay]
parcel il pacco
parcheggio *parking*
pardon *(didn't understand)* come? [*koh*-may]
I beg your pardon *(sorry)* scusi [*skoo*-zee]
parents: my parents i miei genitori [ee mee-*eh*-ee jay-nee-*toh*-ree]
park il parco
where can I park my car? dove posso parcheggiare? [*doh*-vay *pos*-soh par-kay-*jah*-ray]
part la parte [*par*-tay]
partenze *departures*
partner il compagno [kom-*pan*-yoh]
party *(group)* la comitiva [ko-mee-*tee*-vah]
(celebration) la festa
I'm with the . . . party sono con la comitiva di . . . [. . . dee]

pass *(mountain)* il passo
he's passed out è svenuto [eh . . .]
passable *(road)* transitabile
[tran-see-*tah*-bee-lay]
passaggio a livello *level crossing*
passenger il passeggero [pas-say-*jeh*-roh]
passer-by il passante [–tay]
passport il passaporto
past: in the past in passato
see **time**
pastry la pasta
path il sentiero [sen-tee-*eh*-roh]
patient: be patient sia paziente [*see*-ah pa-tzee-*e*n-tay]
pattern il disegno [dee-*say*n-yoh]
pavement il marciapiede [mar-cha-pee-*eh*-day]
pay pagare [pa-*gah*-ray]
can I pay, please? posso pagare, per favore? [. . . fa-*voh*-ray]
peace la pace [*pah*-chay]
peach una pesca
peanuts le arachidi [a-*rah*-kee-dee]
pear una pera [*pay*-rah]
peas i piselli [ee . . .]
pebble il ciottolo [*cho*t-toh-loh]
pedal il pedale [pay-*dah*-lay]
pedestrian il pedone [pay-*doh*-nay]
pedestrian crossing passaggio pedonale [pas-*sah*-joh pay-doh-*nah*-lay]
» *TRAVEL TIP: do not assume that cars will stop or even slow down for you at a pedestrian crossing*
pedoni *pedestrians*
peg *(clothes)* la molletta da bucato [. . . boo-*kah*-toh]
(tent) il picchetto [peek-*kay*t-toh]
pelvis il bacino [ba-*chee*-noh]
pen la penna
have you got a pen? ha una penna? [ah . . .]
pencil la matita [ma-*tee*-tah]

penfriend il corrispondente [–tay]
penicillin la penicillina [pay-nee-cheel-*lee*-nah]
penknife il temperino [–*ree*-noh]
pensioner il pensionato
people la gente [*je*n-tay]
  the Italian people gli Italiani [lee . . .]
pepper il pepe [*pay*-pay]
  (vegetable) il peperone [–nay]
peppermint la menta [m*ay*n-tah]
per per [payr]
  per person/night/week per persona/per notte/per settimana
per cent per cento [. . . ch*e*n-toh]
perfect perfetto
  the perfect holiday la vacanza perfetta [va-k*a*n-tzah . . .]
perfume il profumo [pro-f*oo*-moh]
perhaps forse [f*o*r-say]
pericolo *danger*
pericoloso sporgersi *do not lean out*
period il periodo [pay-*ree*-o-doh]
  (medical) le mestruazioni [mays-troo-a-tzee-*oh*-nee]
perm la permanente [–tay]
permit *(noun)* il permesso
person la persona
  in person in persona
petrol la benzina [ben-tz*ee*-nah]
  petrol station il distributore di benzina [dees-tree-boo-t*oh*-ray dee . . .]
» *TRAVEL TIP: 'normale' = 2 star; 'super' = 4 star*
phone *see* **telephone**
photograph la fotografia [–f*ee*-ah]
  would you take a photograph of us? ci fa la fotografia? [chee . . .]
piano il pianoforte [–tay]
pickpocket il borseggiatore [bor-say-ja-t*oh*-ray]
pie *(sweet)* la torta
  (savoury) il pasticcio [pas-t*ee*-choh]

piece il pezzo [*pe*t-tzoh]
a piece of . . . un pezzo di . . . [. . . dee]
pig il maiale [ma-*yah*-lay]
pigeon il piccione [pee-ch*oh*-nay]
pile-up un incidente a catena [een-chee-*de*n-tay ah . . .]
pill la pillola [*pee*l-lo-lah]
do you take the pill? prendi la pillola?
pillion: on the pillion sul sellino posteriore [sool sel-*lee*-noh pos-tay-ree-*oh*-ray]
pillow il cuscino [koo-sh*ee*-noh]
pin lo spillo [sp*ee*l-loh]
pineapple l'ananas
pink *(adjective)* rosa
pint la pinta [*pee*n-tah]
» *TRAVEL TIP: 1 pint = 0.57 litres*
pipe il tubo [t*oo*-boh]
(smoking) la pipa [*pee*-pah]
pipe tobacco il tabacco da pipa
piston il pistone [–nay]
pity: it's a pity è un peccato [eh . . .]
place il posto
is this place taken? questo posto è occupato?
do you know any good places to go? conosce dei posti interessanti? [ko-n*oh*-shay day *po*s-tee een-tay-rays-s*a*n-tee]
plain *(food)* semplice [*se*m-plee-chay]
(not patterned) senza nessun disegno [*se*n-tzah nays-s*oo*n dee-s*ay*n-yoh]
plane l'aereo [ah-*eh*-ray-oh]
by plane in aereo
plant la pianta [pee-*an*-tah]
plaster *(medical)* il gesso [*je*s-soh]
see **sticking**
plastic la plastica [pl*a*s-tee-kah]
plate il piatto [pee-*a*t-toh]
platform *(rail)* il marciapiede [mar-cha-pee-*eh*-day]
which platform, please? che binario, per

favore? [kay bee-*nah*-ree-oh payr fa-*voh*-ray]
play: somewhere for the children to play un posto dove i bambini possano giocare [. . . *doh*-vay ee bam-*bee*-nee pos-sa-noh jo-*kah*-ray]
pleasant piacevole [pee-a-*chay*-vo-lay]
please per favore [payr fa-*voh*-ray]
could you please . . .? potrebbe . . .? [po-*trayb*-bay]
yes, please sì, grazie [see *grah*-tzee-ay]
pleasure il piacere [pee-a-*chay*-ray]
my pleasure prego [*pray*-goh]
plenty: plenty of . . . un sacco di . . . [. . . dee]
thank you, that's plenty grazie, basta [*grah*-tzee-ay . . .]
pliers le pinze [*peen*-tzay]
plimsolls le scarpe di tela [lay *skar*-pay dee *tay*-lah]
plug *(electrical)* la spina [*spee*-nah]
(car) la candela [–*day*-lah]
(bath) il tappo
» TRAVEL TIP: *you will need 2-pin plugs in Italy*
plum la prugna [*proon*-yah]
plumber l'idraulico [ee-*drow*-lee-koh]
plus più [pew]
p.m. di pomeriggio [dee po-may-*ree*-joh]
pneumonia la polmonite [pol-mo-*nee*-tay]
poached egg un uovo affogato [*wo*-voh . . .]
pocket la tasca
point: could you point to it? me lo può indicare? [may lo pwoh een-dee-*kah*-ray]
four point six quattro e sei [. . . ay say]
points *(car)* le puntine [poon-*tee*-nay]
police la polizia [po-lee-*tzee*-ah]
get the police chiami la polizia [kee-*ah*-mee . . .]
policeman il poliziotto [po-lee-tzee-*ot*-toh]
police station il posto di [dee] polizia
» TRAVEL TIP: *most police duties are carried out by*

the Carabinieri; to contact the police dial 113
polish *(noun)* il lucido [loo-chee-doh]
would you polish my shoes? potrebbe lucidarmi le scarpe? [po-trayb-bay loo-chee-dar-mee lay skar-pay]
polite cortese [kor-tay-say]
politics la politica [po-lee-tee-kah]
polluted inquinato [een-kwee-nah-toh]
polythene bag un sacchetto di plastica [sak-kayt-toh dee plas-tee-kah]
pool *(swimming)* la piscina [pee-shee-nah]
poor: I'm very poor sono molto povero [. . . po-vay-roh]
poor quality di qualità scadente [dee kwa-lee-tah ska-den-tay]
popular popolare [–ray]
population la popolazione [po-po-la-tzee-oh-nay]
pork il maiale [ma-yah-lay]
port *(also drink)* il porto
to port a babordo
porter il facchino [fak-kee-noh]
portrait il ritratto
posh elegante [–tay]
possible possibile [pos-see-bee-lay]
could you possibly . . .? potrebbe . . .? [po-trayb-bay]
post la posta
post box la cassetta delle lettere [–ray]
postcard la cartolina [kar-toh-lee-nah]
post office l'ufficio postale [oof-fee-choh pos-tah-lay]
» *TRAVEL TIP: postal service can be slow*
poste restante il fermo posta
potato la patata
pottery le terraglie [ter-ral-yay]
pound *(sterling)* la lira sterlina [lee-rah ster-lee-nah]
(weight) la libbra [leeb-brah]

» *TRAVEL TIP: conversion:* $\frac{pounds}{11} \times 5 = kilos$

pounds	*1*	*3*	*5*	*6*	*7*	*8*	*9*
kilos	*0.45*	*1.4*	*2.3*	*2.7*	*3.2*	*3.6*	*4.1*

pour: it's pouring sta piovendo a catinelle [stah pee-o-*ven*-doh ah ka-tee-*nel*-lay]
powder la polvere [*pol*-vay-ray]
(face) la cipria [*chee*-pree-ah]
power cut: there's a power cut manca la corrente [–tay]
power point la presa (di corrente) [*pray*-sah dee kor-*ren*-tay]
prawns i gamberi [*gam*-bay-ree]
prawn cocktail un cocktail di [dee] gamberi
prefer: I prefer this one preferisco questo
pregnant incinta [een-*cheen*-tah]
prescription la ricetta [ree-*chet*-tah]
present: at present adesso
here's a present for you eccole un regalo [*ek*-ko-lay . . .]
president il presidente [. . . *den*-tay]
press: could you press these? mi può stirare questi? [mee pwoh stee-*rah*-ray *kwes*-tee]
pretty carino [ka-*ree*-noh]
it's pretty expensive è assai caro [eh as-*sah*-ee . . .]
price il prezzo [*pret*-tzoh]
priest il prete [*preh*-tah]
printed matter stampe [*stam*-pay]
prison la prigione [pree-*joh*-nay]
private privato [pree-*vah*-toh]
probably probabilmente [–tay]
problem il problema
product il prodotto
profit il profitto
promise: do you promise? promette? [–tay]
I promise prometto
pronounce: how do you pronounce

this? come si pronuncia? [k*oh*-may see pro-n*oo*n-chah]
pronto soccorso *first aid*
propeller l'elica [*eh*-lee-kah]
properly per bene [. . . b*ay*-nay]
prostitute una prostituta [pros-tee-t*oo*-tah]
protect proteggere [pro-t*eh*-jay-ray]
Protestant protestante [–t*a*n-tay]
proud orgoglioso [or-gol-y*oh*-soh]
prove: I can prove it posso provarlo
public: the public il pubblico [p*oo*b-blee-koh]
public convenience la toilette [twa-l*e*t]
» *TRAVEL TIP: not as many as in Britain, but most bars have a toilet that can be used free of charge*
public holidays i giorni festivi [j*o*r-nee fes-t*ee*-vee]
» *TRAVEL TIP: public holidays: January 1st ('Capodanno'); Good Friday ('Venerdì Santo'); Easter Monday ('Pasqua'); April 25th; May 1st; August 15th ('l'Assunzione'); November 1st ('Ognissanti'); December 8th ('l'Immacolata Concezione'); December 25th ('Natale'); December 26th ('Santo Stefano')*
pudding il budino [boo-d*ee*-noh]
(dessert) il dolce [d*o*l-chay]
pull *(verb)* tirare [tee-r*ah*-ray]
he pulled out in front of me mi ha tagliato la strada [mee ah tal-y*ah*-toh la str*ah*-dah]
pump la pompa
punctual puntuale [poon-too-*ah*-lay]
puncture una foratura [fo-ra-t*oo*-rah]
pure puro [p*oo*-roh]
purple porpora [p*o*r-po-rah]
purse il borsello
push *(verb)* spingere [sp*ee*n-jay-ray]
pushchair il passeggino [pas-say-j*ee*-noh]
put: where can I put . . .? dove posso mettere . . .? [d*oh*-vay p*o*s-soh m*e*t-tay-ray]
pyjamas il pigiama [pee-j*ah*-mah]

quality la qualità [kwa-lee-*tah*]
quarantine la quarantena [kwa-ran-*tay*-nah]
quarter un quarto [*kwar*-toh]
  a quarter of an hour un quarto d'ora
  see **time**
quay il molo
question una domanda
queue *(noun)* la coda
» *TRAVEL TIP: the queueing habit is not very strong*
quick svelto
  that was quick è stato svelto [eh *stah*-toh . . .]
quiet quieto [kwee-*ay*-toh]
  be quiet! zitto! [*tzeet*-toh]
quite completamente [–tay]
  (fairly) assai [as-*sah*-ee]
  quite a lot un sacco
race *(motor etc)* una corsa
radiator il radiatore [ra-dee-a-*toh*-ray]
radio la radio [*rah*-dee-oh]
rail: by rail col treno
rain la pioggia [pee-*o*-jah]
  it's raining piove [pee-*o*-vay]
  raincoat l'impermeabile
  [eem-per-may-*ah*-bee-lay]
rallentare *slow down*
rally *(car)* il rally
rape lo stupro [*stoo*-proh]
rare raro; *(steak)* al sangue [. . . *san*-gway]
raspberry il lampone [lam-*poh*-nay]
rat un ratto
rather: I'd rather sit here preferisco sedere qui
  [. . . say-*day*-ray kwee]
  I'd rather not preferisco di [dee] no
  it's rather hot fa piuttosto caldo
  [. . . pewt-*tos*-toh . . .]
raw crudo [*kroo*-doh]
razor rasoio [ra-*soh*-yoh]
  razor blades le lamette da barba
  [la-*mayt*-tay . . .]

read: would you read it for me? me lo può leggere? [may loh pwoh *leh*-jay-ray]
something to read qualcosa da leggere
ready: when will it be ready? per quando è pronto? [. . . eh . . .]
I'm not ready yet non sono ancora pronto
real autentico [ow-*ten*-tee-koh]
real leather vera pelle [*vay*-rah pel-lay]
(shoes) vero cuoio [. . . kwo-yoh]
it's a real bargain è un vero affare [eh . . . af-*fah*-ray]
really davvero [dav-*vay*-roh]
rear-view mirror lo specchietto retrovisore [spayk-*yet*-toh ray-tro-vee-*soh*-ray]
reasonable ragionevole [ra-jo-*nay*-vo-lay]
receipt la ricevuta [ree-chay-*voo*-tah]
can I have a receipt, please posso avere la ricevuta, per favore? [*pos*-soh a-*vay*-ray . . . payr fa-*voh*-ray]
recently di recente [dee ray-*chen*-tay]
reception *(hotel)* il ricevimento [ree-chay vee-*men*-toh]
at reception al ricevimento
recipe la ricetta [ree-*chet*-tah]
recommend: can you recommend . . .? può consigliare . . .? [pwoh kon-seel-*yah*-ray]
record *(music)* un disco [*dees*-koh]
red rosso
reduction *(in price)* uno sconto
refuse: I refuse mi rifiuto [mee ree-*few*-toh]
region la regione [ray-*joh*-nay]
registered letter una lettera raccomandata [*let*-tay-rah . . .]
regret: I regret that . . . mi rincresce che . . . [mee reen-*kray* shay kay]
relax: I just want to relax voglio riposarmi [*vol*-yoh ree-po-*sar*-mee]
remember: don't you remember? non si [see] ricorda?

I'll always remember mi ricorderò sempre [mee ree-kor-day-*ro* *se*m-pray]
something to remember you by qualcosa per ricordarti
rent: can I rent a car/boat/bicycle? posso affittare una macchina/barca/bicicletta? [. . . af-feet-*tah*-ray *oo*-nah m*a*k-kee-nah/b*a*r-kah/bee-chee-kl*ay*t-tah]
repair: can you repair it? può ripararlo? [pwoh . . .]
repeat: could you repeat that? può ripetere? [pwoh ree-p*e*h-tay-ray]
reputation la reputazione [ray-poo-ta-tzee-*oh*-nay]
rescue *(verb)* salvare [–ray]
reservation la prenotazione [pray-no-ta-tzee-*oh*-nay]
I want to make a reservation for . . . vorrei fare una prenotazione per . . . [vor-*ray* f*ah*-ray . . .]
reserve: can I reserve a seat? posso prenotare un posto? [. . . pray-no-t*ah*-ray . . .]
responsible responsabile [res-pon-s*ah*-bee-lay]
rest: I've come here for a rest sono venuto qua per riposarmi
you keep the rest tenga il resto
restaurant il ristorante [–tay]
retail price il prezzo al minuto [pr*e*t-tzoh . . .]
retired in pensione [een payn-see-*oh*-nay]
return: a return to . . . un'andata e [ay] *ri*torno per . . .
reverse gear la marcia indietro [m*a*r-chah een-dee-*eh*-troh]
rheumatism il reumatismo [ray-oo-ma-t*ee*s-moh]
rib la costola [k*o*s-toh-lah]
rice il riso [r*ee*-soh]
rich ricco [r*ee*k-koh]
ridiculous ridicolo [ree-d*ee*-ko-loh]

right: that's right è vero [eh-*vay*-roh]
you're right ha ragione lei [ah-ra-*joh*-nay lay]
on the right a destra
right now proprio adesso [*pro*-pree-oh . . .]
(immediately) subito
right here proprio qui [*pro*-pree-oh kwee]
right hand drive la guida a destra [*gwee*-dah ah . . .]
ring *(on finger)* l'anello
ripe maturo [mat-*too*-roh]
rip-off: it's a rip-off è un furto [eh oon *foor*-toh]
riservato *reserved*
river il fiume [*few*-may]
road la strada
which is the road to . . .? qual'è la strada per. . .? [kwa-*leh* . . .]
roadhog un guidatore incosciente [gwee-da-*toh*-ray een-ko-*shen*-tay]
rob: I've been robbed sono stato derubato
rock la roccia [*ro*-chah]
whisky on the rocks un whisky con ghiaccio [ghee-*ah*-choh]
roll *(bread)* un panino [pa-*nee*-noh]
Roman Catholic cattolico [kat-*toh*-lee-koh]
romantic romantico [ro-*man*-tee-koh]
roof il tetto
room la camera [*kah*-may-rah]
have you got a (single/double) room? ha una camera (singola/doppia)? [ah . . . *seen*-go-lah/*dop*-pee-ah]
for one night/for three nights per una notte/per tre notti [. . . *not*-tay]
YOU MAY THEN HEAR . . .
con doccia *with shower*
con bagno *with bath*
spiacenti, ma siamo al completo *sorry, we're full*
room service il servizio [ser-*vee*-tzee-oh]
rope la fune [*foo*-nay]
rose la rosa

rosé rosé
rough *(sea)* agitato
roughly *(approximately)* più o meno [pew o m*ay*-noh]
roulette la roulette
round *(circular)* rotondo
roundabout la rotonda
» *TRAVEL TIP: cars on the roundabout must give way to traffic joining the roundabout*
route: which is the prettiest/fastest route? qual'è la strada più bella/più veloce? [kwa-l*eh* lah str*ah*-dah pew b*e*l-lah/pew vay-l*oh*-chay]
rowing boat una barca a remi [. . . r*ay*-mee]
rubber la gomma
rubber band un elastico [ay-l*a*s-tee-koh]
rubbish una porcheria [por-kay-r*ee*-ah]
(garbage) la spazzatura [spat-tza-t*oo*-rah]
rubbish! sciocchezze! [shok-k*e*t-tzay]
rucksack lo zaino [tza-*ee*-noh]
rudder il timone [tee-m*oh*-nay]
rude maleducato [ma-lay-doo-k*ah*-toh]
ruins le rovine [ro-v*ee*-nay]
rum il rum [room]
rum and coke un rum e coca-cola [. . . ay . . .]
run: hurry, run! corri, fa presto!
I've run out of petrol/money sono rimasto senza benzina/soldi [. . . s*e*n-tzah ben-tz*ee*-nah/s*o*l-dee]
sad triste [tr*ee*s-tay]
safe sicuro [see-k*oo*-roh]
will it be safe here? è al sicuro qua? [eh . . .]
is it safe to swim here? è prudente nuotare qua? [–tay nwo-t*ah*-ray . . .]
safety la sicurezza [see-koo-r*ay*t-tzah]
safety pin la spilla di sicurezza [sp*ee*l-lah dee . . .]
sail le vela [v*ay*-lah]
can we go sailing? possiamo fare [f*ah*-ray]

della barca a vela?
sailor il marinaio [ma-ree-*nah*-yoh]
sala d'aspetto *waiting room*
salad l'insalata
» *TRAVEL TIP: this refers only to vegetables: there is no such thing in Italy as a ham or cheese salad*
salami il salame [–may]
saldi *sale*
sale: is it for sale? è in vendita [eh een *vayn*-dee-tah]
salmon il salmone [sal-*moh*-nay]
salt il sale [*sah*-lay]
same stesso
the same again, please ancora dello stesso, per favore [. . . fa-*voh*-ray]
the same to you altrettanto
sand la sabbia
sandal il sandalo [*san*-da-loh]
sandwich un panino imbottito [pa-*nee*-noh eem-bot-*tee*-toh]
sanitary towels gli assorbenti igienici [lee . . . ee-*jay*-nee-chee]
Sardinia la Sardegna [sar-*dayn*-yah]
satisfactory soddisfacente [sod-dees-fa-*chen*-tay]
Saturday sabato [*sah*-ba-toh]
sauce la salsa
saucepan la casseruola [kas-sayr-*wo*-lah]
saucer il piattino [pee-at-*tee*-noh]
sauna la sauna [*sah*-oo-nah]
sausage la salsiccia [sal-*see*-chah]
save *(life)* salvare [sal-*vah*-ray]
say: how do you say . . . in Italian? come si dice in italiano . . .? [*koh*-may see *dee*-chay . . .]
what did he say? cosa ha detto? [. . . ha . . .]
scala mobile *escalator*
scarf il fazzoletto [fat-tzo-*layt*-toh]
scenery il panorama
schedule il programma

on/behind schedule in orario/in ritardo
scheduled flight il volo di linea [. . . dee *lee*-nay-ah]
school la scuola [skw*o*-lah]
scissors: a pair of scissors un paio di forbici [p*ah*-yoh dee f*o*r-bee-chee]
scooter il motorino [mo-to-r*ee*-noh]
Scotland la Scozia [sk*o*-tzee-ah]
Scottish scozzese [skot-tz*ay*-say]
scrambled eggs le uova strapazzate [lay w*o*-vah stra-pat-tz*ah*-tay]
scratch un graffio [gr*a*f-fee-oh]
scream un grido [gr*ee*-doh]
screw *(noun)* la vite [v*ee*-tay]
screwdriver il cacciavite [ka-cha-v*ee*-tay]
sea il mare [m*ah*-ray]
by the sea al mare
seafood i frutti di mare [ee fr*oo*t-tee dee m*ah*-ray]
search cercare [chayr-k*ah*-ray]
search party squadra il soccorso [skw*ah*-drah dee . . .]
seasick: I get seasick soffro il mal di mare [. . . dee m*ah*-ray]
I feel seasick ho il mal di mare [o . . .]
seaside la spiaggia [spee-*ah*-jah]
let's go to the seaside andiamo al mare [. . . m*ah*-ray]
season la stagione [sta-j*oh*-nay]
in the high/low season in alta/bassa stagione
seasoning il condimento
seat un posto a sedere [. . . say-d*ay*-ray]
is this somebody's seat? è occupato questo posto?
seat belt la cintura di sicurezza [cheen-t*oo*-rah dee see-koo-r*ay*t-tzah]
seaweed le alghe [*a*l-gay]
second secondo
just a second un secondo

second hand di seconda mano [dee . . .]
secret: it's a secret è un segreto [eh . . .]
see vedere [vay-*day*-ray]
I see *(understand)* ho capito [o ka-*pee*-toh]
have you seen . . .? ha visto . . .? [ah . . .]
can I see the room? posso vedere la camera?
seem sembrare [saym-*brah*-ray]
it seems so pare di sì [*pah*-ray dee see]
seldom raramente [ra-ra-*men*-tay]
self: self-service il self-service
self-catering apartment un appartamento con l'uso cucina
sell vendere [*vayn*-day-ray]
send spedire [spay-*dee*-ray]
sensitive sensibile [sen-*see*-bee-lay]
sentimental sentimentale [–*tah*-lay]
separate *(adjective)* separato [say-pa-*rah*-toh]
I'm separated sono diviso [. . . dee-*vee*-soh]
can we pay separately? possiamo avere conti separati? [. . . a-*vay*-ray . . .]
September settembre [–bray]
serious serio [*seh*-ree-oh]
I'm serious sul serio
this is serious questo è grave [. . . *grah*-vay]
is it serious, doctor? è grave, dottore?
service: the service was excellent/poor il servizio era eccellente/lasciava a desiderare [ser-*vee*-tzee-oh *eh*-rah ay-chayl-*len*-tay/la-*shah*-vah ah day-see-day-*rah*-ray]
service station la stazione di servizio [sta-tzee-*oh*-nay dee . . .]
serviette il tovagliolo [to-val-*yo*-loh]
several diversi [dee-*ver*-see]
sexy sexy
shade: in the shade all'ombra
shake scuotere [*skwo*-tay-ray]
to shake hands stringere la mano [*streen*-jay-ray lah *mah*-noh]

» *TRAVEL TIP: customary to shake hands each time you meet somebody and when you take your leave of somebody*
shallow basso
shame: what a shame! che peccato! [kay . . .]
shampoo *(noun)* lo shampoo [sh*a*m-poh]
  shampoo and set shampoo e messa in piega [. . . pee-*ay*-gah]
shandy birra e limonata [b*ee*r-rah ay . . .]
» *TRAVEL TIP: beer is lager-type*
share *(room, table)* dividere [dee-v*ee*-day-ray]
shark lo squalo [skw*ah*-loh]
sharp *(pain)* acuto [a-k*oo*-toh]
  (blade) affilato
  (taste) acido [*ah*-chee-doh]
  (bend) stretto
shave radersi [r*ah*-dayr-see]
  shaver un rasoio [ra-s*oh*-yoh]
  shaving point la presa per il rasoio
  shaving foam schiuma da barba [sk*ew*-mah . . .]
she lei [lay]
  she is è [eh]
sheep la pecora [p*eh*-ko-rah]
sheet il lenzuolo [len-tzw*o*-loh]
shelf lo scaffale [skaf-f*ah*-lay]
shell la conchiglia [kon-k*ee*l-yah]
  shellfish i molluschi [ee mol-l*oo*s-kee]
shelter *(noun)* un riparo
  can we shelter here? possiamo ripararci qua? [. . . ree-pa-r*a*r-chee . . .]
sherry lo sherry
shin la tibia [t*ee*-bee-ah]
ship la nave [n*ah*-vay]
  by ship con la nave
shirt la camicia [ka-m*ee*-chah]
shock *(noun: surprise)* lo shock
  I got an electric shock from the . . . ho preso la scossa con . . . [o . . .]

shock-absorber l'ammortizzatore [am-mor-teet-tza-*toh*-ray]
shoe la scarpa
» *TRAVEL TIP: shoe sizes*

UK	*4*	*5*	*6*	*7*	*8*	*9*	*10*	*11*
Italy	*37*	*38*	*39*	*41*	*42*	*43*	*44*	*46*

shop il negozio [nay-go-tzee-oh]
I've some shopping to do devo fare delle compere [*day*-voh *fah*-ray *del*-lay *kom*-pay-ray]
» *TRAVEL TIP: shops usually close for lunch between 12.30 and 3.30 in winter, 12.30 and 4.30 in summer, and remain open till 7 or 8 p.m.*
shore la costa
on the shore sulla spiaggia [*sool*-lah spee-*ah*-jah]
short corto
I'm three short me ne mancano tre [may nay *man*-ka-noh tray]
short cut la scorciatoia [skor-cha-*toh*-yah]
shorts i calzoncini [ee kal-tzon-*chee*-nee]
shoulder la spalla
shout *(verb)* gridare [gree-*dah*-ray]
show: please show me mi può mostrare? [mee pwoh mos-*trah*-ray]
shower: with shower con doccia [*doh*-chah]
shrimps i gamberetti
shrink: it's shrunk si è ristretto [see . . .]
shut *(verb)* chiudere [kee-*oo*-day-ray]
when do you shut? a che ora chiudete? [ah kay *oh*-rah kee-oo-*day*-tay]
shut up! sta'zitto! [stah-*tzeet*-toh]
shy timido [*tee*-mee-doh]
si prega di non . . . *please do not . . .*
Sicily la Sicilia [see-*cheel*-yah]
sick malato [ma-*lah*-toh]
I feel sick mi sento male [mee *sen*-toh *mah*-lay]
he's been sick è stato male [eh *stah*-toh . . .]
side il lato [*lah*-toh]

side light la luce di posizione [loo-chay dee po-see-tzee-*oh*-nay]
side street una laterale [–lay]
by the side of the road sul margine della strada [sool m*a*r-jee-nay . . .]
sight: out of sight fuori vista [fw*oh*-ree v*ee*s-tah]
we'd like to go on a sightseeing tour vorremmo fare una gita turistica [. . . f*ah*-ray *oo*-nah j*ee*-tah too-r*ee*s-tee-kah]
sign *(notice)* il cartello
signal: he didn't signal non ha indicato [non ah een-dee-k*ah*-toh]
signature la firma
signore *ladies*
signori *gentlemen*
silence *(noun)* il silenzio [see-l*e*n-tzee-oh]
silencer il silenziatore [see-len-tzee-a-t*oh*-ray]
silk la seta [s*ay*-tah]
silly sciocco [sh*o*k-koh]
silver l'argento [ar-j*e*n-toh]
similar simile [s*ee*-mee-lay]
simple semplice [s*ay*m-plee-chay]
since: since last week dalla settimana scorsa
since we arrived da quando siamo arrivati
(because) poiché [poy-k*a*y]
sincere sincero [seen-ch*ay*-roh]
yours sincerely cordiali saluti
sing cantare [kan-t*a*h-ray]
single: single room una camera singola [k*ah*-may-rah s*ee*n-go-lah]
I'm single non sono sposato
a single to . . . un'andata per . . . [oon an-d*ah*-tah . . .]
sink: it sank è affondato
sir signore [seen-y*oh*-ray]
sister: my sister mia sorella [m*ee*-ah . . .]
sit: can I sit here? posso sedermi qui? [. . . say-d*ay*r-mee kwee]

size *(clothes)* la taglia [*ta*l-yah]
(shoes) il numero [*noo*-may-roh]
ski *(noun)* lo sci [shee]
(verb) sciare [shee-*ah*-ray]
skiing lo sciare
ski boots gli scarponi da sci [lee skar-*poh*-nee dah shee]
ski lift la sciovia [shee-o-*vee*-ah]
ski pants i pantaloni da sci [pan-ta-*loh*-nee . . .]
ski pole la racchetta da sci [rak-*kay*t-tah . . .]
ski slope/ski run la pista da sci [*pee*s-tah . . .]
ski wax la sciolina [shee-o-*lee*-nah]
skid sbandare [sban-*dah*-ray]
skin la pelle [*pe*l-lay]
skin diving il nuoto subacqueo [*nwo*-toh soo-*bah*-kway-oh]
» *TRAVEL TIP: see* **aqualung**
skirt la gonna
sky il cielo [*chay*-loh]
in the sky in cielo
sledge la slitta
sleep: I can't sleep non riesco a dormire [. . . ree-*ay*s-koh ah dor-*mee*-ray]
sleeper *(rail)* il vagone letto [va-*goh*-nay . . .]
sleeping bag il sacco a pelo
sleeping pill un sonnifero [sonn-*nee*-fay-roh]
YOU MAY HEAR . . .
ha dormito bene? *did you sleep well?*
sleeve la manica [*mah*-nee-kah]
slide *(photo)* una diapositiva [dee-a-po-see-*tee*-vah]
slow: could you speak a little slower? può parlare un po' più lentamente? [pwoh par-*lah*-ray oon po pew len-ta-*mayn*-tay]
small piccolo
small change la moneta [mo-*nay*-tah]
smell: there's a funny smell c'è un odore strano [chay oon o-*doh*-ray . . .]

it smells puzza [p*oo*t-tzah]
smile *(verb)* sorridere [sor-r*ee*-day-ray]
smoke *(noun)* il fumo [f*oo*-moh]
do you smoke? fuma?
can I smoke? posso fumare? [. . . foo-m*ah*-ray]
smooth liscio [l*ee*-shoh]
snack spuntino [spoon-t*ee*-noh]
can we just have a snack? non vorremmo un pasto completo
snake una serpe [–pay]
snorkel un respiratore [–t*oh*-ray]
snow *(noun)* la neve [n*ay*-vay]
so: it's so hot fa così caldo [. . . ko-s*ee* . . .]
not so much non così tanto
so-so così-così
soap il sapone [sa-p*oh*-nay]
soap powder il detersivo [day-tayr-s*ee*-voh]
sober non ubriaco [. . . oo-bree-*ah*-koh]
socks i calzini [kal-tz*ee*-nee]
soda (water) l'acqua di [dee] soda
soft drink un analcolico [a-nal-k*o*-lee-koh]
sole *(shoe)* la suola [sw*oh*-lah]
could you put new soles on these? può risuolarmi queste? [pwoh ree-swo-l*a*r-mee kw*e*s-tay]
YOU MAY THEN HEAR . . .
di cuoio o di gomma? *leather or rubber?*
some: some people alcune persone [al-k*oo*-nay per-s*oh*-nay]
can I have some? posso averne un po'? [. . . a-v*ay*r-nay . . .]
can I have some grapes/some bread? posso avere dell'uva/del pane? [. . . a-v*ay*-ray del-l*oo*-vah/del p*ah*-nay]
can I have some more? posso averne ancora [. . . a-v*ay*r-nay . . .]
that was some meal! però che pranzo [pay-r*o* kay pr*a*n-tzoh]
somebody qualcuno [kwal-k*oo*-noh]

something qualcosa
sometimes a volte [ah *vo*l-tay]
somewhere da qualche parte [. . . kw*a*l-kay p*a*r-tay]
son: my son mio figlio [m*ee*-oh f*ee*l-yoh]
song una canzone [kan-tz*oh*-nay]
soon presto
as soon as possible appena possibile [. . . pos-s*ee*-bee-lay]
sooner prima [pr*ee*-mah]
sore: it's sore mi fa male [mee fah m*ah*-lay]
sore throat il mal di gola [. . . dee . . .]
sorry: (I'm) sorry mi spiace [mee spee-*ah*-chay]
sort: this sort questo tipo [. . . t*ee*-poh]
what sort of . . .? che tipo di . . .? [kay t*ee*-poh dee]
will you sort it out? ci pensa lei? [chee p*e*n-sah lay]
sosta autorizzata (9–12) *parking (between 9 and 12)*
sosta vietata *no waiting*
sottopassaggio *underpass*
soup la zuppa [tz*oo*p-pah]
south sud [sood]
South Africa il Sudafrica [soo-d*ah*-free-kah]
South African sudafricano
souvenir un souvenir
spade la vanga
(child's) la paletta
spaghetti gli spaghetti [lee spa-g*ay*t-tee]
spanner la chiave inglese [kee-*ah*-vay een-gl*ay*-say]
spare: spare part il pezzo di ricambio [p*e*t-tzoh dee ree-k*a*m-bee-oh]
spare wheel la ruota di scorta [rw*o*-tah dee . . .]
spark(ing) plug la candela
speak: do you speak English? parla l'inglese? [. . . leen-gl*ay*-say]

I don't speak Italian non parlo l'italiano
special speciale [spay-*chah*-lay]
specialist lo specialista [spay-cha-*lees*-tah]
specially specialmente [spay-chal-*mayn*-tay]
spectacles gli occhiali da vista [lee ok-*yah*-lee . . .]
speed la velocità [vay-lo-chee-*tah*]
he was speeding aveva superato il limite di velocità [. . . *lee*-mee-tay dee . . .]
speed limit il limite di velocità
speedometer il tachimetro [ta-*kee*-may-troh]
spend *(money)* spendere [*spen*-day-ray]
spices le spezie [*spet*-zee-ay]
is it spicy? è piccante? [eh peek-*kan*-tay]
it's too spicy è troppo piccante
spider il ragno [*ran*-yoh]
spingere *push*
spirits le bevande alcoliche [lay bay-*van*-day al-*ko*-lee-kay]
spoon il cucchiaio [kook-*yah*-yoh]
sprain *(noun)* una storta
I've sprained my ankle ho preso una storta alla caviglia [o . . . ka *veel*-yah]
spring la molla
(season) la primavera [pree-ma-*veh*-rah]
square *(in town)* la piazza [pee-*at*-tzah]
two square metres due metri quadri [*doo*-ay . . .]
stairs le scale [lay *skah*-lay]
stall: it keeps stalling non fa altro che fermarsi [. . . kay . . .]
stalls *(theatre)* la platea [pla-*teh*-ah]
stamp il francobollo [fran-ko-*bol*-loh]
two stamps for Britain, please due francobolli per l'Inghilterra, per favore [*doo*-ay . . . payr leen-gheel-*ter*-rah, payr fa-*voh*-ray]
» *TRAVEL TIP: buy stamps at tobacconists and most bars*

stand *(verb)* stare in piedi [st*ah*-ray een pee-*eh*-dee]
(at fair) lo stand
standard *(adjective)* medio [m*e*d-yoh]
standard model un modello standard
stand-by di riserva [dee . . .]
star una stella
starboard tribordo [tree-b*o*r-doh]
start: my car won't start la macchina non parte [m*a*k-kee-nah non p*a*r-tay]
when does it start? quando comincia? [kw*a*n-doh ko-m*ee*n-chah]
starter *(car)* il motorino d'avviamento [mo-to-r*ee*-noh dav-vee-a-m*ay*n-toh]
starving: I'm starving sto morendo di fame [. . . dee f*ah*-may]
station la stazione [sta-tzee-*oh*-nay]
statue la statua [st*ah*-too-ah]
stay: we enjoyed our stay abbiamo avuto un soggiorno piacevole [ab-bee-*ah*-moh a-v*oo*-toh oon so-j*or*-noh pee-a-ch*ay*-vo-lay]
stay there resta lì [. . . lee]
I'm staying at . . . sono al . . .
steak la bistecca [bees-t*ay*k-kah]
YOU MAY HEAR . . .
al sangue [al s*a*n-gway] *rare*
poco cotta *medium rare*
cotta bene [. . . b*ay*-nay] *well done*
steep ripido [r*ee*-pee-doh]
steering *(car)* lo sterzo [st*ay*r-tzoh]
steering wheel il volante [–tay]
step *(stairs)* il gradino [gra-d*ee*-noh]
stereo stereo
sterling *(pound)* la sterlina [stayr-l*ee*-nah]
stewardess la hostess
sticking plaster il cerotto [chay r*o*t-toh]
sticky appiccicoso [ap-pee-chee-k*oh*-soh]
stiff rigido [r*ee*-jee-doh]
still *(adjective)* calmo [k*a*l-mo]

keep still sta' fermo
I'm still here sono ancora qui
stink *(noun)* una puzza [poot-tzah]
stolen: my wallet's been stolen mi hanno rubato il portafoglio [mee-*a*n-noh roo-b*ah*-toh eel por-ta-f*o*l-yoh]
stomach lo stomaco [st*o*-ma-koh]
I've got stomach-ache ho il mal di stomaco [o eel mal dee . . .]
have you got something for an upset stomach? ha qualcosa per il mal di stomaco? [ah . . .]
stone la pietra [pee-eh-trah]
» *TRAVEL TIP: 1 stone = 6.35 kilos*
stop: stop! ferma!
stop-over la fermata
do you stop near . . .? si ferma vicino . . .? [see f*e*r-mah vee-ch*ee*-noh ah]
storm il temporale [taym-po-r*ah*-lay]
straight diritto [dee-r*ee*t-toh]
go straight on sempre diritto [s*e*m-pray . . .]
straight away subito [s*oo*-bee-toh]
straight whisky un whisky liscio [l*ee*-shoh]
strange strano
stranger un estraneo [es-trah-nay-oh]
I'm a stranger here non sono pratico del luogo [. . . pr*ah*-tee-koh del lw*o*-goh]
strawberry la fragola [fr*ah*-go-lah]
street la strada
string: have you got any string? ha della corda? [ah . . .]
striptease lo striptease
stroke: he's had a stroke gli è venuto un attacco [lee eh vay-n*oo*-toh . . .]
strong forte [f*o*r-tay]
student uno studente [stoo-d*e*n-tay]
stung: I've been stung sono stato punto [. . . p*oo*n-toh]
stupid stupido [st*oo*-pee-doh]

such: such a lot così tanto [ko-*see* . . .]
suddenly improvvisamente [–tay]
sugar lo zucchero [tz*oo*-kay-roh]
suit *(man's)* l'abito [*ah*-bee-toh]
(woman's) il tailleur [ta-*yoor*]
suitcase una valigia [va-*lee*-jah]
suitable adatto
summer l'estate [es-*tah*-tay]
sun il sole [*soh*-lay]
in the sun al sole
out of the sun all'ombra
sunbathe prendere il sole [*pren*-day-ray . . .]
sunburn la scottatura [skot-ta-*too*-rah]
sunglasses gli occhiali da sole [lee ok-*yah*-lee . . .]
suntan oil l'olio solare [*lol*-yoh so-*lah*-ray]
sunstroke il colpo di [dee] sole
Sunday domenica [doh-*may*-nee-kah]
suonare *please ring*
supermarket il supermercato
supper la cena [*chay*-nah]
sure: I'm not sure non sono sicuro [see-*koo*-roh]
sure! certamente! [chayr-ta-*mayn*-tay]
are you sure? è sicuro? [eh . . .]
surfboard la tavola da surfing
surfing: to go surfing andare a fare il surfing [an-*dah*-ray ah *fah*-ray eel . . .]
surname il cognome [kon-*yoh*-may]
swear word una parolaccia [pa-ro-*lah*-chah]
sweat *(verb)* sudare [soo-*dah*-ray]
sweet: it's too sweet è troppo dolce [eh . . . *dol*-chay]
(dessert) il dolce
sweets caramelle [–lay]
swerve: I had to swerve ho dovuto deviare improvvisamente [o do-*voo*-toh day-vee-*ah*-ray eem-prov-vee-sa-*men*-tay]
swim: I'm going for a swim vado a fare una nuotata [*vah*-doh ah *fah*-ray *oo*-nah

nwo-*tah*-tah]
swimming costume il costume da bagno [kos-*too*-may dah *ban*-yoh]
swimming pool la piscina [pee-*shee*-nah]
Swiss svizzero [*sveet*-tzay-roh]
Switzerland la Svizzera [*sveet*-tzay-rah]
switch *(noun)* l'interruttore [een-ter-root-*toh*-ray]
to switch (something) on/off accendere/spegnere (qualcosa) [a-*chen*-day-ray/*spen*-yay-ray . . .]
table la tavola [*tah*-vo-lah]
a table for 4 un tavolo per quattro
table wine un vino da pasto [*vee*-noh . . .]
take prendere [*pren*-day-ray]
can I take this with me? posso prendere questo?
will you take me to the airport? mi può condurre all'aeroporto? [mee pwoh kon-*door*-ray al-la-ay-ro-*por*-toh]
how long will it take? quanto ci vorrà? [. . . chee . . .]
somebody has taken my bags qualcuno ha preso le mie valigie [. . . ah *pray*-soh lay *mee*-ay va-*lee*-jay]
can I take you out tonight? posso portarti fuori questa sera? [. . . *fwoh*-ree . . .]
is this seat taken? è occupato? [eh . . .]
talcum powder il borotalco
talk *(verb)* parlare [par-*lah*-ray]
tall alto
tampons i tamponi [ee tam-*poh*-nee]
tan l'abbronzatura [ab-bron-tza-*too*-rah]
I want to get a tan voglio abbronzarmi [*vol*-yoh ab-bron-*tzar*-mee]
tank *(of car)* il serbatoio [sayr-ba-*toh*-yoh]
tap il rubinetto [roo-bee-*nayt*-toh]
tape il nastro
tape recorder il registratore

[ray-jees-tra-*toh*-ray]
tariff la tariffa
taste *(noun) (food)* il sapore [sa-*poh*-ray]
(clothes etc) il gusto [*goo*s-toh]
can I taste it? posso assaggiare?
[as-sa-*jah*-ray]
it tastes horrible/very nice fa schifo/è molto buono [fah sk*ee*-foh/eh m*o*l-toh bw*o*-noh]
taxi il tassì [tas-*see*]
will you get me a taxi? mi può chiamare un tassì? [mee pwoh kee-a-m*ah*-ray . . .]
where can I get a taxi? dove posso prendere un tassì? [d*oh*-vay p*o*s-soh pr*e*n-day-ray . . .]
taxi-driver il tassista
tea il tè [teh]
could I have some tea? posso avere un tè?
[. . . a-v*ay*-ray . . .]
tea with milk/with lemon tè al latte/al limone [. . . l*a*t-tay/al lee-m*oh*-nay]
teapot una teiera [tay-yeh-rah]
» *TRAVEL TIP: tea is usually served either black or with lemon ('al limone'); tea with milk is very unusual and milk must be ordered separately*
teach: could you teach me? mi può insegnare?
[mee pwoh een-sayn-*yah*-ray]
teacher l'insegnante [een-sayn-*ya*n-tay]
telegram il telegramma
I want to send a telegram vorrei spedire un telegramma [vor-r*ay* spay-d*ee*-ray . . .]
telephone *(noun)* il telefono [tay-l*eh*-fo-noh]
can I make a phone-call? posso fare una telefonata? [. . . f*ah*-ray . . .]
can I speak to . . .? posso parlare con . . .?
[. . . par-l*ah*-ray . . .]
could you get this number for me? mi può chiamare questo numero? [mee pwoh kee-ah-m*ah*-ray kw*e*s-toh n*oo*-may-roh]
telephone directory l'elenco telefonico
[. . . tay-lay-f*o*-nee-koh]

» *TRAVEL TIP: for public phones you'll need tokens (gettoni), 1 for local, min. of 6 for international calls; buy gettoni at tobacconists, bars, post offices, newsagents; code for UK is 0044 and drop first 0 of UK area code; in larger towns go to SIP where the assistant will put you through*

television la televisione [tay-lay-vee-see-*oh*-nay]
I'd like to watch television vorrei guardare la televisione [vor-*ray* gwar-*dah*-ray . . .]
tell: could you tell me where . . .? mi può dire dove . . .? [mee pwoh *dee*-ray *doh*-vay]
temperature *(weather etc)* la temperatura [–*too*-rah]
he's got a temperature ha la febbre [ah lah *feb*-bray]
temporary temporaneo [–*rah*-nay-oh]
tenere la destra *keep right*
tennis il tennis
tennis court il campo da tennis
tennis racket la racchetta da tennis [rak-*kay*t-tah . . .]
tennis ball la palla da tennis
tent la tenda
terminus il capolinea [ka-po-*lee*-nay-ah]
terrible terribile [ter-*ree*-bee-lay]
terrific magnifico [man-*yee*-fee-koh]
than di [dee]
bigger/older than . . . più grande/più vecchio di . . . [pew *gran*-day/pew *vek*-yoh dee]
thanks, thank you grazie [*grah*-tzee-ay]
no thank you no grazie
thank you very much grazie tante [. . . *tan*-tay]
thank you for your help grazie per l'aiuto
YOU MAY THEN HEAR . . .
prego *you're welcome*
that quello

that man/that table quell'uomo/quella tavola [kwayl-wo-moh/kw*ay*l-lah t*ah*-vo-lah]
I would like that one vorrei quello [vor-r*ay* . . .]
how do you say that? come si dice? [k*oh*-may see d*ee*-chay]
the *(singular)* il, lo; la
(plural) i [ee], gli [lee]; le [lay]
theatre il teatro [tay-*ah*-troh]
their il loro; la loro
it's their bag/it's theirs è la loro borsa/è loro
them loro
I see them li vedo [lee v*ay*-doh]
then allora
there lì [lee]
how do I get there? come ci arrivo? [k*oh*-may chee ar-r*ee*-voh]
is there . . ./are there . . .? c'è . . ./ci sono . . .? [cheh/chee s*oh*-noh]
there is . . ./there are . . . c'è . . ./ci sono . . .
there you are *(giving something)* ecco
these questi
these apples queste mele [. . . m*ay*-lay]
can I take these? posso prendere questi? [. . . pr*e*n-day-ray . . .]
they essi [*e*s-see]
they are sono
thick spesso; *(stupid)* duro [d*oo*-roh]
thief il ladro
thigh la coscia [k*oh*-shah]
thin sottile [sot-t*ee*-lay]
thing una cosa
I've lost all my things ho perso tutto quello che avevo [o p*e*r-soh t*oo*t-toh kw*ay*l-loh kay a-v*ay*-voh]
think pensare [pen-s*ah*-ray]
I'll think it over ci penso su [chee . . . soo]
I think so/I don't think so penso di sì/di no [p*e*n-soh dee see . . .]

third *(adjective)* terzo [*tay*r-tzoh]
thirsty: I'm thirsty ho sete [o *say*-tay]
this questo
this hotel/this street quest'albergo/questa strada
can I have this one? posso avere questo?
this is my wife/this is Mr . . . questa è mia moglie/questo è il signor . . . [. . . m*ee*-ah m*o*l-yay . . ./eel seen-y*o*r . . .]
is this . . .? è questo . . . [eh . . .]
those quelli; quelle [kw*ay*l-lee kw*ay*l-lay]
how much are those? quanto costano? [. . . k*o*s-ta-noh]
thousand mille [m*ee*l-lay]
thousands migliaia [meel-*yah*-yah]
thread *(noun)* il filo [f*ee*-loh]
three tre [tray]
throat la gola [g*oh*-lah]
throttle l'acceleratore [a-chay-lay-ra-t*oh*-ray]
through attraverso
through there per di là [. . . dee lah]
throw *(verb)* gettare [jet-t*ah*-ray]
thumb il pollice [p*o*l-lee-chay]
thunder *(noun)* il tuono [tw*oh*-noh]
thunderstorm il temporale [–r*ah*-lay]
Thursday giovedì [jo-vay-d*ee*]
ticket il biglietto [beel-y*e*t-toh]
(cloakroom) lo scontrino [skon-tr*ee*-noh]
» *TRAVEL TIP: see* **bus**
tie *(necktie)* la cravatta
tight *(clothes)* stretto
they're too tight sono troppo stretti
tights il collant [ko-l*o*ng]
time il tempo
what's the time? che ore sono? [kay *oh*-ray . . .]
I haven't got time non ho tempo [. . . o . . .]
for the time being per ora
this time/last time/next time questa volta/la

volta scorsa/la prossima [pros-see-mah] volta
3 times tre volte [tray-vol-tay]
have a good time! si diverta! [see dee-ver-tah]
timetable l'orario [o-rah-ree-oh]
» *TRAVEL TIP: how to tell the time*
it's one o'clock è l'una [eh loo-nah]
it's two/three/four o'clock sono le due/tre/quattro [lay doo-ay/tray . . .]
it's 5/10/20/25 past seven sono le sette e cinque/dieci/venti/venticinque [set-tay ay cheen-kway/dee-*eh*-chee/vayn-tee/vayn-tee-cheen-kway]
it's quarter past eight/eight fifteen sono le otto e un quarto/le otto e quindici [. . . kween-dee-chee]
it's half past nine/nine thirty sono le nove e mezza/le nove e trenta [. . . no-vay ay met-tzah . . .]
it's 25/20/10/5 to ten sono le dieci meno venticinque/venti/dieci/cinque [. . . may-noh . . .]
it's quarter to eleven/10.45 sono le undici meno un quarto/le dieci e quarantacinque [oon-dee-chee . . .]
it's twelve o'clock (am/pm) sono le dodici (di mattina/di notte) [. . . d*oh*-dee-chee . . .–tay]
at one o'clock all'una
at three thirty alle tre e trenta
tin *(can)* un barattolo [ba-rat-toh-loh]
tin-opener l'apriscatole [a-pree-sk*ah*-toh-lay]
tip *(noun)* la mancia [man-chah]
is the tip included è compresa la mancia? [eh . . .]
» *TRAVEL TIP: same people as in UK*
tirare *pull*
tired stanco
I'm tired sono stanco
tissues i fazzolettini di carta [ee fat-tzoh-let-tee-nee dee . . .]
to: to Rome/England a Roma/in Inghilterra

[. . . een-gheel-*ter*-rah]
toast il pane tostato [*pah*-nay tos-*tah*-toh]
(drinking) un brindisi [*bree*n-dee-see]
» *TRAVEL TIP: 'toast' or 'tosti' in Italy are toasted sandwiches available as a snack in most bars*
tobacco il tabacco
tobacconist's il tabaccaio [ta-bak-*kah*-yoh]
» *TRAVEL TIP: stamps can be bought here*
today oggi [*o*-jee]
toe il dito del piede [*dee*-toh del pee-*eh*-day]
together insieme [een-see-*ay*-may]
we're together siamo insieme [see-*ah*-moh . . .]
can we pay all together? possiamo pagare tutti insieme? [. . . pa-*gah*-ray . . .]
toilet la toilette [twa-*let*]
where are the toilets? dove sono le toilette [*doh*-vay *soh*-noh lay twa-*let*]
I have to go to the toilet devo andare al gabinetto [*day*-voh an-*dah*-ray . . .]
there's no toilet paper non c'è carta igienica [non cheh *kar*-tah ee-*jay*-nee-kah]
» *TRAVEL TIP: see* **public convenience**
tomato un pomodoro
tomato ketchup il ketchup
tomato juice il succo di pomodoro [*soo*k-koh dee . . .]
tomorrow domani [dom-mah-nee]
tomorrow morning/tomorrow afternoon/tomorrow evening domattina/domani pomeriggio [. . . po-may-*ree*-joh]/domani sera
the day after tomorrow dopodomani
see you tomorrow a domani
ton una tonnellata
» *TRAVEL TIP: 1 ton = 1,016 kilos*
tongue la lingua [*lee*n-gwah]
tonic (water) l'acqua brillante [. . . breel-*la*n-tay]

tonight stasera [stah-*say*-rah]
tonne una tonnellata
» *TRAVEL TIP: 1 tonne = 1000 kilos = metric ton*
tonsils le tonsille [ton-*seel*-lay]
tonsillitis la tonsillite [–*lee*-tay]
too troppo
(also) anche [an-kay]
that's too much questo è troppo [. . . eh . . .]
tool un attrezzo [at-*tret*-tzoh]
tooth un dente [*den*-tay]
I've got toothache ho mal di denti [o . . . dee *den*-tee]
toothbrush lo spazzolino da denti [spat-tzo-*lee*-noh . . .]
toothpaste il dentifricio [den-tee-*free*-choh]
top: on top of sopra
on the top floor all'ultimo piano [al-*lool*-tee-moh pee-ah-noh]
at the top in cima [een *chee*-mah]
total *(noun)* il totale [toh-*tah*-lay]
tough *(meat)* duro [*doo*-roh]
tour *(noun)* un viaggio [vee-*ah*-joh]
we'd like to go on a tour of . . . vorremmo visitare . . . [. . . vee-see-*tah*-ray]
we're touring around facciamo il giro del paese [fa-*chah*-moh eel *jee*-roh del pah-*ay*-say]
tourist un turista
I'm a tourist sono un turista
tourist office l'ufficio turistico [oof-*fee*-choh too-*rees*-tee-koh]
tow *(verb)* rimorchiare [ree-mor-kee-*ah*-ray]
can you give me a tow? mi può rimorchiare? [mee pwoh . . .]
towrope un cavo da rimorchio [*kah*-voh dah ree-*mor*-kee-oh]
towards verso
he was coming straight towards me veniva diritto verso di me [vay-*nee*-vah dee-*reet*-toh *ver*-soh dee may]

towel un asciugamano [a-shoo-ya-m*ah*-noh]
town la città [cheet-t*ah*]
in town in città
would you take me into the town? mi porta in città? [mee . . .]
traditional tradizionale [tra-dee-tzee-o-n*ah*-lay]
a traditional Italian meal un pasto all'italiana
traffic il traffico [tr*a*f-fee-koh]
traffic lights il semaforo [say-m*ah*-fo-roh]
» TRAVEL TIP: *traffic lights are often suspended over junctions, so watch out for this*
traffic policeman il vigile [v*ee*-jee-lay]
train il treno
» TRAVEL TIP: *best to book in advance as trains are crowded; 'rapido' is fast intercity, often first-class only, surcharge payable*
tranquillizers i tranquillanti [–tee]
translate tradurre [tra-door-ray]
would you translate that for me? me lo può tradurre? [may lo pwoh . . .]
transmission *(of car)* la trasmissione [tras-mees-y*oh*-nay]
travel agent's l'agenzia di viaggi [a-jen-tz*ee*-ah dee vee-*ah*-jee]
traveller's cheque il traveller's cheque
tree l'albero [*a*l-bay-roh]
tremendous formidabile [–d*ah*-bee-lay]
trim: just a trim please solo una spuntatina per favore [. . . spoon-ta-t*ee*-nah . . .]
trip *(noun)* un viaggio [vee-*ah*-joh]
we want to go on a trip to . . . vorremmo fare una gita a . . . [. . . f*ah*-ray *oo*-nah j*ee*-tah ah]
trouble *(noun)* un disturbo [dees-t*oo*r-boh]
I'm having trouble with the steering/my back ho delle noie allo sterzo/dei disturbi alla schiena [o d*e*l-lay n*o*-yay *a*l-loh st*ay*r-tzoh/day dees-t*oo*r-bee *a*l-lah skee-*ay*-nah]

trousers i pantaloni
true vero [*vay*-ro]
it's not true non è vero [. . . eh . . .]
trunks *(swimming)* il costume [kos-too-may]
trust: I trust you ho fiducia in lei [o fee-*doo*-chah een lay]
try *(verb)* provare [pro-*vah*-ray]
please try provi per favore [*pro*-vee payr fa-*voh*-ray]
can I try it on? posso provarlo?
T-shirt una maglietta [mal-*yay*t-tah]
Tuesday martedì [mar-tay-*dee*]
turn: where do we turn off? dove voltiamo? [*doh*-vay vol-tee-*ah*-moh]
he turned without indicating ha voltato senza indicare [ah . . . *se*n-tzah een-dee-*kah*-ray]
twice due volte [*doo*-ay *vo*l-tay]
twice as much il doppio [*do*p-pee-oh]
twin beds due letti [*doo*-ay *le*t-tee]
two due [*doo*-ay]
typewriter la macchina da scrivere [*ma*k-kee-nah dah skr*ee*-vay-ray]
typical tipico [*tee*-pee-koh]
tyre la gomma
I need a new tyre ho bisogno di una nuova gomma [o bee-*so*nn-yoh dee *oo*-nah nw*o*-vah . . .]

» *TRAVEL TIP: tyre pressures*

lb/sq in	*18*	*20*	*22*	*24*	*26*	*28*	*30*
kg/sq cm	*1.3*	*1.4*	*1.5*	*1.7*	*1.8*	*2*	*2.1*

ugly brutto [br*oo*t-toh]
ulcer l'ulcera [ool-ch*ay*-rah]
Ulster l'Ulster [*oo*l-ster]
umbrella l'ombrello
uncle lo zio [tz*ee*-oh]
uncomfortable scomodo [sk*o*-mo-doh]
unconscious inconscio [een-k*o*n-shoh]

under sotto
underdone poco cotto
underground *(rail)* la metropolitana
understand: I understand capisco
I don't understand non capisco
do you understand? capisce? [ka-*pee*-shay]
undo disfare [dees-*fah*-ray]
unfriendly scontroso
unhappy infelice [een-fay-*lee*-chay]
United States gli Stati Uniti [lee *stah*-tee oo-*nee*-tee]
unlock aprire [a-*pree*-ray]
until fino a [*fee*-noh ah]
not until non prima di [. . . dee]
unusual insolito [een-*so*-lee-toh]
uomini *gentlemen*
up su [soo]
he's not up yet non si è ancora alzato [non see eh an-*koh*-rah al-*tzah*-toh]
what's up? cosa succede? [. . . soo-*chay*-day]
upside down alla rovescia [. . . ro-*veh*-shah]
to turn upside down capovolgere [ka-po-*vol*-jay-ray]
upstairs di sopra [dee . . .]
urgent urgente [oor-*jen*-tay]
us: it's not for us non è per noi [. . .eh payr *no*-ee]; **can you help us?** può aiutarci? [pwoh ah-yoo-*tar*-chee]
uscita *exit*
use: can I use . . .? posso adoperare . . .? [*rah*-ray]
useful utile [*oo*-tee-lay]
usual solito [*so*-lee-toh]
as usual come al solito [*koh*-may . . .]
usually di solito [dee . . .]
U-turn un'inversione [een-vers-*yoh*-nay]
vacancy: do you have any vacancies? avete una camera libera? [a-*vay*-tay *oo*-nah *kah*-may-rah *lee*-bay-rah]

vacate *(room)* lasciare vacante [la-sh*ah*-ray va-k*a*n-tay]
vaccination la vaccinazione [va-chee-na-tzee-*oh*-nay]
vacuum flask il thermos [t*ay*r-mos]
valanghe *avalanches*
valid valido [v*ah*-lee-doh]
how long is it valid for? fino a quando è valido? [f*ee*-noh ah . . .]
valuable di valore [dee va-l*oh*-ray]
my valuables i miei oggetti di valore [ee mee-*eh*-ee o-j*e*t-tee . . .]
value *(noun)* valore [va-l*oh*-ray]
valve la valvola [v*a*l-vo-lah]
vanilla la vaniglia [va-n*ee*l-yah]
varicose veins le vene varicose [v*ay*-nay va-ree-k*oh*-say]
veal il vitello [vee-t*e*l-loh]
vegetables le verdure [vayr-d*oo*-ray]
vegetarian *(noun)* un vegetariano [vay-jay-ta-ree-*ah*-noh]
ventilator il ventilatore [–t*oh*-ray]
vernice fresca *wet paint*
very molto
very much moltissimo
via via [v*ee*-ah]
vietato fumare *no smoking*
village il villaggio [veel-l*ah*-joh]
vine la vite [v*ee*-tay]
vinegar l'aceto [a-ch*ay*-toh]
vineyard la vigna [v*ee*n-yah]
vintage l'annata
violent violento [vee-o-l*e*n-toh]
visibility la visibilità [–t*ah*]
visit *(verb)* visitare [vee-see-t*ah*-ray]
vodka la vodka
voice la voce [v*oh*-chay]
voltage il voltaggio [vol-t*ah*-joh]
waist la vita [v*ee*-tah]

» *TRAVEL TIP: waist measurements*
UK 24 26 28 30 32 34 36 38
Italy 61 66 71 76 80 87 91 97

wait: will we have to wait long? dobbiamo aspettare a lungo? [. . . as-payt-*tah*-ray ah *loo*n-goh]
wait for me mi aspetti [mee . . .]
I'm waiting for a friend/my wife aspetto un amico/mia moglie [. . . oon a-*mee*-koh/*mee*-ah-*mo*l-yay]

waiter il cameriere [ka-may-ree-*eh*-ray]
waiter! cameriere!

waitress la cameriera [ka-may-ree-*eh*-rah]
waitress! cameriera!

wake: will you wake me at 7.30? mi sveglia alle sette e mezza [mee *sve*l-yah *a*l-lay *se*t-tay ay *me*t-tzah]

Wales il Galles [*ga*l-lays]

walk: can we walk there? possiamo andarci a piedi? [. . . an-*da*r-chee ah pee-*eh*-dee]
are there any good walks around here? ci sono delle belle passeggiate qua? [chee *so*h-noh *de*l-lay *be*l-lay pas-say-*jah*-tay kwa]
walking shoes le scarpe da passeggio [lay *ska*r-pay dah pas-*say*-joh]
walking stick il bastone da passeggio [bas-*toh*-nay . . .]

wall il muro [*moo*-roh]
(inside) la parete [pa-*ray*-tay]

wallet il portafoglio [por-ta-*fo*l-yoh]

want: I want a . . . voglio un . . . [*vo*l-yoh oon]
I want to talk to . . . voglio parlare con . . . [. . . par-*lah*-ray . . .]
what do you/does he want? che cosa vuole? [kay-*ko*-sah *vwo*-lay]
I don't want to non ne ho voglia [non nay o *vo*l-yah]

warm caldo

warning l'avviso [av-*vee*-soh]

was: I was/he was ero/era [*eh*-roh . . .]
it was era
wash: can you wash these for me? può lavarmi questi? [pwoh . . .]
where can I wash? dove mi posso lavare? [d*oh*-vay mee . . . la-v*ah*-ray]
where can I wash this? dove posso lavare questo?
washing machine la lavatrice [la-va-tr*ee*-chay]
washing powder il detersivo [day-tayr-s*ee*-voh]
washer *(for nut & bolt)* la rondella
wasp la vespa
watch *(wrist-)* l'orologio [o-ro-l*oh*-joh]
will you watch my bags for me? può guardarmi i bagagli? [pwoh gwar-d*a*r-mee ee ba-g*a*l-yee]
watch out! attento!
water l'acqua
can I have some water? posso avere dell'acqua? [. . . a-v*ay*-ray . . .]
hot and cold running water acqua corrente calda e fredda [. . . kor-r*e*n-tay . . .]
waterproof impermeabile [eem-per-may-*ah*-bee-lay]
waterskiing lo sci nautico [shee n*ow*-tee-koh]
way: we'd like to eat the Italian way vorremmo mangiare all'italiana [. . . man-j*ah*-ray . . .]
could you tell me the way to . . .? mi può indicare la strada per . . .? [mee pwoh een-dee-k*ah*-ray . . .]
see **where** *for answers*
we noi [n*o*-ee]
we are siamo [see-*ah*-moh]
weak *(person)* debole [d*ay*-bo-lay]
weather il tempo

what filthy weather! che tempo schifoso! [kay *te*m-poh skee-*foh*-soh]
what's the weather forecast? quali sono le previsioni del tempo? [kw*ah*-lee *soh*-noh lay pray-vee-see-*oh*-nee . . .]
YOU MAY THEN HEAR . . .
pioverà [pee-o-vay-*rah*] *it is going to rain*
farà bel tempo [fa-*rah* . . .] *it's going to be fine*
Wednesday mercoledì [mer-ko-lay-*dee*]
week la settimana
a week today oggi a otto [*o*-jee . . .]
at the weekend al weekend
weight il peso
well: I'm not feeling well non mi sento bene [non mee *se*n-toh *bay*-nay]
he's not well non sta bene
how are you? – very well, thanks come sta? – bene, grazie [*koh*-may stah – *bay*-nay gr*ah*-tzee-ay]
you speak English very well parla un buon inglese [. . . bwon een-gl*ay*-say]
wellingtons gli stivali di gomma [lee stee-v*ah*-lee dee . . .]
Welsh gallese [gal-l*ay*-say]
were: you were era [*eh*-rah]
(familiar) eri
(plural) eravate [eh-ra-v*ah*-tay]
we were eravamo
they were erano [*eh*-ra-noh]
west ovest [*o*-vest]
West Indies le Indie Occidentali [*ee*n-dee-ay o-chee-dayn-t*ah*-lee]
wet bagnato [ban-y*ah*-toh]
(weather) umido [*oo*-mee-doh]
wet suit la tuta da sub [t*oo*-tah dah soob]
what cosa
what is that? cos'è questo? [koh-s*eh* . . .]
what for? perché [payr-k*ay*]
wheel la ruota [rw*o*-tah]

when quando
when is breakfast? a che ora è la colazione? [ah kay *oh*-rah eh lah ko-la-tzee-*oh*-nay]
where dove [d*oh*-vay]
where is the post office? dov'è l'ufficio postale? [doh-v*eh* loof-f*ee*-choh pos-t*ah*-lay]
YOU MAY THEN HEAR . . .
diritto *straight on*
a destra *to the right*
a sinistra *to the left*
torni in dietro *go back*
which quale [kw*ah*-lay]
which one? quale
YOU MAY THEN HEAR . . .
questo *this one* quello *that one*
whisky il whisky
white bianco [bee-*a*n-koh]
Whitsun la Pentecoste [–tay]
who chi [kee]
wholesale all'ingrosso
whose di chi [dee kee]
whose is this? di chi è questo?
YOU MAY THEN HEAR . . .
è mio *it's mine*
è suo *it's his/it's hers*
why perché [payr-k*a*y]
why not? perché no?
wide largo
wife: my wife mia moglie [m*ee*-ah m*o*l-yay]
will: when will it be finished? quando sarà pronto?
will you do it? lo fa lei? [. . . lay]
I will come back tomorrow torno domani
wind *(noun)* il vento
window la finestra [fee-n*e*s-trah]
near the window vicino alla finestra [vee-ch*ee*-noh . . .]
windscreen il parabrezza [pa-ra-br*ay*t-tzah]
windscreen wipers i tergicristalli [ee

tayr-jee-krees-*ta*l-lee]
windy: it is windy today oggi c'è vento [o-jee cheh *ve*n-toh]
wine il vino [*vee*-noh]
can I see the wine list? posso avere la lista dei vini? [. . . a-*vay*-ray lah *lee*s-tah day *vee*-nee]
» *TRAVEL TIP: best wines show D.O.C. (Denominazione d'Origine Controllata) and the place where bottled (cantine di . . .) on the label;*
Barolo, Barbera, Barbaresco *full-bodied reds from Piedmont, go well with roasts and venison;*
Bardolino, Valpolicella *light reds, go well with all kinds of meat;*
Pinot Bianco/Grigio *dry whites from Friuli;*
Lambrusco *sparkling red from Emilia;*
Frascati *white, dry or sweet, from near Rome;*
Chianti *red and white, from Tuscany, (the best is Chianti Classico);*
Verdicchio *dry white from Marche, very good with fish;*
Vernaccia *dry white from Sardinia, very strong and aromatic*
winter l'inverno
wire il filo metallico [*fee*-loh may-*ta*l-lee-koh]
(electrical) il filo eletrico
wish: best wishes tanti auguri
with con
without senza [*se*n-tzah]
witness testimone [tes-tee-*moh*-nay]
will you act as a witness for me? mi può fare da testimone? [mee pwoh *fah*-ray . . .]
woman la donna
women le donne [*do*n-nay]
wonderful meraviglioso [may-ra-veel-*yoh*-soh]
won't: it won't start non parte [–tay]
wood *(trees)* il bosco
it's made of wood è di legno [eh di *lay*n-yoh]
wool la lana
word la parola

I don't know that word non conosco quella parola

work *(verb)* lavorare [la-vo-*rah*-ray]

it's not working non funziona [. . . foon-tzee-*oh*-nah]

I work in London lavoro a Londra

worry: I'm worried about him sono preoccupato per lui [. . . *loo*-ee]

don't worry non si preoccupi

worse: it's worse è peggio [eh *peh*-joh]

he's getting worse sta peggiorando [stah pay-jo-*ran*-doh]

worst il peggio [*peh*-joh]

worth: it's not worth that much non vale tanto [. . . *vah*-lay . . .]

is it worthwhile going to . . .? vale la pena di andare a . . .? [*vah*-lay lah *pay*-nah dee an-*dah*-ray ah]

wrap: could you wrap it up? mi può fare un pacchetto? [mee pwoh *fah*-ray oon pak-*kayt*-toh]

wrench *(noun: tool)* la chiave inglese [kee-*ah*-vay een-*glay*-say]

wrist il polso

write scrivere [*skree*-vay-ray]

could you write it down? può scriverlo? [pwoh . . .]

I'll write to you ti scrivo [tee *skree*-voh]

writing paper la carta da lettere [. . . *let*-tay-ray]

wrong sbagliato [sbal-*yah*-toh]

I think the bill's wrong penso che il conto sia sbagliato

there's something wrong with . . . c'è qualcosa che non va con . . . [cheh kwal-*ko*-sa kay . . .]

you're wrong lei ha torto [lay ah *tor*-toh]

sorry, wrong number scusi, ho sbagliato numero [*skoo*-zee, o sbal-*yah*-toh *noo*-may-roh]

X-ray una radiografia [ra-dee-o-gra-*fee*-ah]
yacht lo yacht
yard *(measurement)* una iarda [*ya*r-dah]
» *TRAVEL TIP: 1 yard = 91.44 cm = 0.91 m*
year l'anno
this year/next year quest'anno/l'anno prossimo [. . . *pro*s-see-moh]
yellow giallo [*ja*l-loh]
yes sì [see]
yesterday ieri [*yeh*-ree]
the day before yesterday l'altroieri [al-tro-*yeh*-ree]
yesterday morning/afternoon ieri mattina/ieri pomeriggio [. . . po-may-*ree*-joh]
yet: is it ready yet? è già pronto? [eh djah . . .]
not yet non ancora
yoghurt lo yoghurt
you lei [lay]
(familiar) tu [too]
(plural) voi [*vo*-ee]
I can't hear you non la/ti/vi sento [. . . tee vee . . .]
I'll send it to you glielo spedisco [lee-*ay*-loh . . .]/te lo spedisco [tay . . .]/ve lo spedisco [vay . . .]
with you con lei/te/voi
is that you? è lei/sei tu/siete voi? [eh lay/say too/see-*ay*-tay *vo*-ee]
» *TRAVEL TIP: only use the 'tu' form with good friends*
young giovane [*joh*-va-nay]
your suo [*soo*-oh]; tuo [*too*-oh]; vostro
see **you**
is this your camera, is this yours? è questa la sua/tua macchina fotografica, è sua/tua questa? [eh . . . *ma*k-kee-nah photo-*grah*-fee-kah . . .]
youth hostel l'ostello per la gioventù [. . . jo-ven-*too*]

Yugoslavia la Jugoslavia [yoo-go . . .]
Yugoslavian jugoslavo
zero zero [tz*eh*-roh]
below zero sotto zero
zip la cerniera [chayr-nee-*eh*-rah]
zona disco *parking disc zone*

The Italian Alphabet

letters in brackets don't actually exist in the Italian alphabet but are useful for spelling English names etc

a [ah]
b [bee]
c [chee]
d [dee]
e [ay]
f [effay]
g [gee]
h [akka]
i [ee]
(j) [ee lunga]
(k) [kappa]
l [ellay]
m [emmay]
n [ennay]
o [oh]
p [pee]
q [koo]
r [erray]
s [essay]
t [tee]
u [oo]
v [voo]
(w) [voo doppio]
(x) [eeks]
(y) [ee-greka]
z [tzay-tah]

Numbers

0 zero [tzay-roh]

1 uno [*oo*-noh]	**6** sei [say]
2 due [d*oo*-ay]	**7** sette [s*e*t-tay]
3 tre [tray]	**8** otto
4 quattro	**9** nove [n*o*-vay]
5 cinque [ch*ee*n-kway]	**10** dieci [dee-*eh*-chee]

11 undici [*oo*n-dee-chee]
12 dodici [d*oh*-dee-chee]
13 tredici [tr*ay*-dee-chee]
14 quattordici [kwat-t*o*r-dee-chee]
15 quindici [kw*ee*n-dee-chee]
16 sedici [s*ay*-dee-chee]
17 diciassette [dee-chas-s*e*t-tay]
18 diciotto [dee-ch*o*t-toh]
19 diciannove [dee-chan-n*o*-vay]

20 venti	**21** ventuno
22 ventidue	**23** ventitré
24 ventiquattro	**25** venticinque
26 ventisei	**27** ventisette
28 ventotto	**29** ventinove

30 trenta	**31** trentuno
40 quaranta	**50** cinquanta
60 sessanta	**70** settanta
80 ottanta	**90** novanta

100 cento [ch*e*n-toh]
101 centouno [chen-toh-*oo*-noh]
165 centosessantacinque
200 duecento
1000 mille [m*ee*l-lay]
2000 duemila [doo-ay-m*ee*-lah]